NECESSARY
CONVERSATIONS

T0056838

NECESSARY
CONVERSATIONS

Between Families and Their Aging Parents

Second Edition

Gerald W. Kaufman
and L. Marlene Kaufman

New York, New York

Library of Congress Cataloging-in-Publication Data available on file.

ISBN: 978-1-68099-181-9
eBook ISBN: 978-1-68099-184-0

Cover design by Jane Sheppard
Cover image by iStockphotos

Printed in the United States of America

Table of Contents

Preface

In this second edition of *Necessary Conversations*, we strive to preserve the most essential ideas of our previous book while adding new insights gained since the original book was released. Daily, or so it seems, we meet people with new stories, challenges, and successes. We continue to learn of progress being made in the understanding of aging and of interventions that can be helpful. The subject is very fluid.

It is still our passion that seniors need to form a team with younger family members and/or friends around the time of their retirement to plan for and to manage the changes that are coming. If that window has been missed, it is important to get started promptly. The team will consult with the senior's physician, lawyer, financial advisor, and perhaps clergy. The wellbeing of the senior is a mission that they all share.

Since the release of the first edition of *Necessary Conversations*, we have been asked to speak at many places across the country and in Canada. Aging has become an important theme perhaps because so many persons are living longer. This longevity has important implications, including those that are financial, medical, housing, familial, and societal in nature. We cannot afford to ignore any of them. Unfortunately, many of us avoid facing these subjects and only involve family members or friends when we are in a crisis. Then, the choices may not be the best ones and can be financially, emotionally, medically, and relationally painful.

One of the most challenging and perplexing choices pertains to end-of-life care. With the support of families or friends, increasing numbers of seniors, while still competent, are deciding to avoid medical intervention when their death or profound mental impairment are certain and irreversible. More people are beginning to understand the consequences of artificially postponing death.

What, then, have we learned about aging from new sources as well as from the groups and individuals we have met with over the last several years?

1. It is now common for seniors to have no adult children, or if they have some, the children live too far away to be meaningfully involved in their care. Because of this, we have expanded the language of caregiving beyond adult children to include other relatives and even non-family helpers.

2. Families that have long-term conflict find it difficult to work together as a team. The conflict may be between the parents, between parents and adult children, among the adult children, or even among niece and nephew caregivers.

3. Some seniors find it difficult to surrender control while others don't want to "be a burden on anyone."

4. Many adult children or substitutes don't feel comfortable moving into a collegial role with a senior. Some find it hard to think about their loved one declining, and others simply don't have enough time or interest to assume this responsibility.

5. Many seniors and their caregivers *are* having productive conversations. There is a developing awareness in the public mind that changes are needed in the ways we address aging. This is enabling more people to enter the conversation. Some are using resources like our book to help them get started.

In light of these realities, we felt an update was important. On the one hand, we want to give voice to the many people who are already making good decisions about aging. We could fill a book with their stories. On the other hand, we want to acknowledge the seniors who, for one reason or another, find it difficult to get the conversations started. In this edition, we attempt to address these concerns. The process of aging is a conversation that must continue between seniors and the people who support them and within the broader community. None of us should get old alone!

In the midst of writing this edition of *Necessary Conversations*, two of our closest friends developed life threatening diseases (cancer and vascular dementia). As their illnesses advanced, neither chose life-extending treatment. They, with the support of their families, made decisions that allowed them to spend their remaining time celebrating each day as a special gift. Adult children, grandchildren, and friends came to their bedside, laughed, cried, and affirmed each other for the years they had together. Death came gently and as a natural extension of life. In the midst of their pain and grief, these families demonstrated a model for living and dying that enlightens all of us. They did not die alone.

We give special words of thanks to the many people who read our original book or participated in our seminars and are committed to dealing with aging in a positive way. The stories you have told us, the questions you have raised, and the constructive ways you have challenged us have been very helpful. We are learning together. We are especially grateful to persons who have allowed us to use/reuse their personal stories. They are inspiring and informing.

Since our previous book was released, we became aware of Dr. Glenn Miller's book, *Living Thoughtfully, Dying Well*. He tells his personal story of facing his own mortality and finding meaning in his life. We are committed to a common mission.

Also, we are grateful to Dr. Ken Brubaker, a geriatric physician who emphasizes palliative care in his teaching and in his practice. He reviewed our chapter on health and offered some important new resources and perspectives. We especially absorbed his passion about the need to challenge the *medicalization of aging* that many seniors are confronted with.

In addition, our knowledge base has been expanded with the help of Dr. Thomas Miller, palliative care and hospice director. He also reviewed our chapter on health and, together with his wife Jill, a hospice nurse, has given us a more complete understanding of death and dying. They also put us in touch with some useful resources that we were able to use in this edition of the book.

Finally, a big shout-out to our editor, Chamois Holschuh, who took on our project with energy, conviction, and with a joyful spirit. Her suggestions have been most helpful. Thanks to Good Books and Skyhorse Publishing for agreeing to share our ideas.

—Gerald W. Kaufman and L. Marlene Kaufman

Beginning the Conversations

MOM: *You know, last night when we went out to dinner and they asked if we wanted the senior discount, I just about said "no." Really, were you ready for that? Seniors! We're not old yet. Why do they have to rush the calendar? I want to stay young as long as I can.*

DAD: *Taking a senior discount doesn't make you old. We're only old if we think we are. Besides, who doesn't want discounts these days? We can get better rates at motels, concerts, and lots of other places. Look, we don't have to even think of being old for another twenty years, so don't lose any sleep over some little discount.*

DAUGHTER: *Mom called today and was upset because they were offered a senior discount at a restaurant last night. She was embarrassed—maybe even offended. She's not ready to think about being old. Now every time they go out, she says it's staring them in the face. Are they* *going to be confronted with this discount thing? I tried to tell her how young she looks and how everybody their age goes through the same thing, but I don't think she's convinced.*

SON: *I'll call Mom and get her straightened out. There's no need for her to be so upset about such a small thing. They shouldn't be so uptight about their age. I don't know what their plans are for the future, but at their age, it isn't a big deal now. They should be happy for the discounts. Besides, we have plenty of our own things to worry about.*

AUNT: *Sometimes when I think about the future, I get concerned. Being single and having no children, it seems like I'm going to have to face a lot of changes by myself. I know that sixty-five isn't old and that I should have many good years ahead of me. And I've always been independent and haven't had to lean on anybody. I know my niece is busy, but maybe she'd be willing to support me if I need help.*

NIECE: *I saw Auntie at the store this week, and she seemed happy about being retired. But I saw just a bit of worry in her eyes when she talked about the years ahead. It must be hard not having her own children to turn to. I don't want her to get old alone. I know she's always done well and has prided herself on being independent. I think I should talk with her.*

The best time to plant a tree is twenty years ago. The next best time is today.

—African proverb

As we approach our senior years, many of us don't think much about the changes that are coming. At the moment, they seem far away. At this time, most of us are in good health and active, and things are going well. So our thoughts center on cruises, golf, hobbies, and perhaps most of all, the freedom to do nothing if that is what we choose. When a *what-if* thought crosses our mind, we quickly push it aside, telling ourselves that we'll deal with it when we have to. But for now, it's "let the good times roll."

Thinking about the future, though, is important to do now. And beyond thinking, we need to begin the conversations now. For some of us, the talking is with our spouse, and if we have adult children, it includes them. But for those of us who have no spouse or adult children, we need to turn to a niece or nephew, or to a younger trusted friend to partner with us on our journey. Whatever our arrangement, we will form a team that also includes our lawyer, financial advisor, physician, and perhaps our clergy person to plan for our future. None of us should get old alone, and all of us need to plan for what is ahead of us.

We need other persons to support us because there are too many unknowns as we get older. Some are too difficult to handle by ourselves. However, some surveys indicate that only about one-third of parents have talked with their adult children about the future, and if they have, it didn't happen until the parents were in a crisis.[1] Seniors without children rarely seek the counsel of others. Unfortunately, some medical crises may make it impossible to convey our wishes, causing decisions to be made for us.

The best time to begin these conversations is around the time of retirement when most of us are still in good health and competent. Statistics indicate that, if we live until age sixty-five, 70 percent of us will reach our eighty-fifth birthday.[2] The possibility that we could live for twenty or more years makes it even more important to begin these conversations early.

Among many other things, we should talk about our finances, health and safety, where we might want to live, and how we want to be cared for when our health declines. It is especially important to talk about end-of-life decisions. Most of all, we want these conversations to be ongoing because our needs and wishes will change as we age.

Living in a complex world

These conversations need to happen because we live in a world that is becoming increasingly complex. Barry Schwartz, in his book *The Paradox of Choice*, graphically illustrates the challenges that come to Americans at all ages when confronted with choice-making about unlimited products and options, including those in the world of high tech. For seniors, this challenge can be overwhelming especially because of their diminishing abilities. It is well known that they are susceptible to scams, risky investments, and even being manipulated by friends and relatives. Seniors can also be influenced to give money beyond their means, even to worthy causes. Because of these challenges, it is imperative that we have a support system in place to help us make the right choices.

Our resistance to asking for help

There are many reasons that some of us don't initiate these conversations with the partners who could help us. Among other things, we don't want to burden them during a very demanding time in their own lives. They are often feeling pressure from their careers or from raising their families. Also, asking for their help can appear to be a sign of weakness on our part. We want to hide that as long as possible. If we have adult children for our partners, we may resist inviting them to help us because many of us are influenced by parenting theories that we learned when they were younger. These theories emphasized the importance of not placing too many demands on them. Author Lori Gottlieb says that parents were encouraged to give their children the freedom to find themselves and to pursue anything they wanted in life. The term "individuation" was used to illustrate an alternative to the dreaded state of "co-dependency." It inferred that having any obligation to care for each other was somehow pathological. So now, when we need them, it may be hard to change that pattern.

It may come as a surprise then to read in an AARP study that 70 percent of our adult children are still receiving some financial support from us.[3] In addition, a recent Pew Research Center study revealed that 36.4 percent of women between the ages of eighteen and thirty-four still lived with parents or relatives in 2014. For men, the percentage was even higher: 42.8. If our adult children are dependent in this way, can we expect them to become partners during our time of need?

One of the biggest challenges that many of us have comes from not allowing *anyone* to help us. We don't want to give up our independence. Throughout our adult lives, we have prided ourselves on being self-sufficient. Most of us had careers that were significant and satisfying. We were active in our community and may have been leaders in a variety of ways. Most of all, we made decisions by ourselves. So as we enter this phase of our lives, it is hard to shift gears. In the back of our minds, the word "dependency" is accompanied by the words "decline," "disability," "dementia," and "death." These things are too unpleasant to think about, so we put off the discussion for another time.

Readiness

When we do choose our partners, it is important that they are mature enough to be comfortable in their role. Starting too early can create problems. Marion and Verna found that out when—in their fifties—they attempted to prepare their son and daughter—then in their twenties—for what would happen if Marion and Verna died suddenly. The urgency to start this discussion was driven by the fact that both had lost their mothers at a young age. They didn't want their children to be unprepared for this situation. However, the children were not ready to face that idea, so they postponed the discussion until the children were older. Next time they revisited the subject, it went well.

There are other reasons that some parents and adult children have trouble talking. For some, it is because they experienced conflict with each other in earlier years. Perhaps we can't begin the family conversations because the adult children have conflicts among themselves. Some of us are just uncomfortable talking about anything personal. Too many of us don't get started because we are procrastinators.

Some parents don't take the initiative because their own parents were not good conversation role models and tended to keep their thoughts to themselves. Many of our parents never talked with their parents about aging because life expectancy back then was much shorter, and there was much less to plan for. Some had a sense of fatalism.

Now that most of us are living much longer, it is time to create a new model for purposeful conversations. We need to invite teammates to begin partnering with us. We and our team must work together to ensure the best possible outcomes and to begin talking about the changes that are ahead of us. When we are in our sixties and seventies, it is likely that we will need less help from our teammates. Most of us are in good health, independent, and self-managed.

One of the teammate's roles, though, will be to accompany us to the various professionals who serve us. That should put all of us in a good position to deal with the losses that do happen during this period. Most of all, this will prepare our teammates for the inevitable changes that come in the later years. Too many of us only begin to deal with crisis planning after the fact, and that can be costly both financially and emotionally.

Facing an unwelcome life stage

Planning for this life stage isn't something we look forward to because, for the first time in our lives, we are entering a stage that we *don't* want to be in. Few people—if any— actually want to get old.

That is very much in contrast to our earlier life stages. As toddlers, we wanted to walk. In fact, our parents said we ran before we walked! Later, we were excited about starting school. When we became adolescents, we couldn't wait to drive. After graduating from high school, many of us eagerly anticipated attending college, starting careers, getting married, having children, buying homes, and traveling. But now we are entering a stage that few of us look forward to and know that there is nothing we can do to stop it from happening.

Societal influences

We push off these thoughts because we are surrounded by a culture that is obsessed with staying young. The messages that come to us imply that delaying aging is an option. We see images in the media of seniors who are enjoying vibrant lives. They are dancing the night away, rafting on white water, and sitting in bathtubs by the ocean. Advertisements encourage us to take medications to correct every age-related infirmity. None of the models used in those ads are hunched over or in wheelchairs. Cosmetic surgeons promise to take away our wrinkles and reshape our bodies. The messages suggest that changing the outside will also change the inside. These voices of denial in culture even shape the language we use. No one is old; we are just "senior citizens," and the time we are living in is always "golden." Euphemisms have a way of numbing us to the many realities that are a part of aging—at least for a time.

In some ways, we are still young

On the other hand, there is some truth to the fact that we *are* younger than our parents were at this age. For many of us, seventy is the new sixty. Generally, we are healthier, and we think and act younger than our parents did. Instead of being incapacitated, housebound seventy-year-olds, many of us are traveling the world and engaging in activities that we didn't have time for earlier. We take up new hobbies or expand old ones. We audit courses at local colleges, and many of us find new meaning through volunteering.

Some of us are kept more youthful by staying active with our grandchildren. Increasingly, we engage in exercise programs that keep our bodies and minds sharp. More of us are enjoying our work so much that we put off our retirement; others choose new careers or work part-time. All of these activities have a profound effect on how we age. This allows some of us to believe that we will never get old.

This sense of immortality has been aided by advances in medical care. Instead of being invalids due to damaged knees or hips, we can remain mobile by having joint replacements. Many of us have another lease on life after heart surgery. We have medications that help control blood pressure, diabetes, and cholesterol. Our lives are extended through various cancer treatments. So not only are we living longer, our quality of life is better. In some ways, we really *are* younger.

With this sense of immortality, we may choose lifestyles that suggest that we will be around for a long time. We build large homes to accommodate our many possessions, create significant estates, and make long-term plans. We are a part of a powerful generation that made enormous changes in our world. We put a man on the moon and now believe that nothing can stop us from going to Mars. The new frontier is ours to explore and to conquer. Aging can't possibly get in our way.

But, then we begin to ask ourselves: What will we do if our net worth declines? Will our stock market investments take a hit? Will our pension plan remain sound? Will there be enough money to pay for long-term care? Some of us still carry significant debt and worry about how to manage on a fixed income. In order to survive financially, we may even need to work longer than planned. When we face these unpleasant thoughts, our world begins to feel less secure.

Learning from the past and other cultures
As we look around our neighborhoods, we begin to observe the many continuing-care communities that are being

developed or expanded. We wonder who will care for us when our health declines. Will it be possible to remain in our own home? Indeed, aging at home was the standard practice in the past and is common among various ethnic and religious groups even today.

When I (Marlene) was a young child, my seventy-year-old grandfather came to live with my family after his second wife died. My parents and eight siblings warmly welcomed him. He brought humor with his storytelling and was a positive influence on our family. He was never an intrusion and was an active part of the family life. I have good memories of him helping to peel peaches and watching him trim the grape vines. He died at our home at age eighty-four. My mother was his primary caregiver.

That pattern is present in various ethnic communities in North America and around the world. While serving as relief workers in Vietnam, Mark and his family observed the interaction of three-generation families in their courtyards. From the balcony, he often saw grandparents sitting among their grandchildren as they played. The parents were working as professionals in the city.

Don and Anna Ruth Jacobs, who spent more than twenty years as missionaries in Africa, found seniors being cared for—and valued—within the family in what are called *mji* in Swahili, or "family villages." Lawrence Chiles, a bishop in the Koinonia Fellowship of Churches, also observed that, in African families he visited, there is a great deal of respect shown for the elderly. He says the Swahili term to describe the relationship children have with the elderly is *shikamoo,* meaning "I grasp your feet." The response of the elder, though, is *marahaba*—"Don't overdo it." Children bow low when they greet their elders as a sign of respect.

In the African American community in the United States, Lawrence says the church plays an important role in setting the tone for relationships among generations. Many congregations have a "mother of the church," who serves as a disciplinarian for the children and even as an unofficial advisor to the pastor. Three-generation households are common. It is expected that elderly parents will be cared for within the home of one of their children.

Lawrence's wife, Nereida, grew up in a Hispanic home where her mother cared for her elderly mother for eleven years, and later for her father. When Nereida thought about her own future, she worried that she would become a burden on her children. However, when Lawrence and Nereida told their three adult children that they were considering moving to a continuing-care community in the future, the children all responded, "Don't even give it a thought. We will take care of you when that time comes!" Their response came as a pleasant surprise. The children also expressed concern about their parents' adjustment to retirement.

In a similar way, Tony and his wife, Dorothy, talked with their four children about planning for their future. He grew up in Puerto Rico and remembered that his sister took care of their parents until they died, but he wondered if his children would do the same for them. He was aware of the cultural shift in family life that was happening in the Hispanic community in the States and doubted that his four busy children would have the time to care for them. However, all expressed a commitment to welcome them into their homes and to provide care as long as possible.

Within the Amish and some Mennonite groups, it is also assumed that adult children will care for their parents. Parents rarely go to nursing homes. Many Amish build a small apartment, called a "grossdawdy house," attached to the main house. Others like John and Mary build a smaller house just up the hill but on the property of one of the children. Even though they aren't living in the same house, they are close enough to allow daily contact with their family. Several other adult children and their families are just a short carriage ride away. John and Mary are clearly part of a family village. John helps his son on the farm, and Mary and the women of the family work together to preserve food from their gardens. John and Mary have a large room in the basement to accommodate their children and grandchildren for meals.

Within this "village," Amish values of simple living and separation from the surrounding culture encourages families to stay connected as they move through life stages. This makes it possible for them to reject Social Security and Medicare. Almost no older Amish members live in nursing care facilities. This network cares for seniors in their homes, including aunts and uncles who have no children. Adult children share in caregiving, and those who live far away make extended visits when it is their turn.

Realities in the creation of a support team

While we can learn from other models, all seniors will encounter some challenges that are unique to their situation. They and their support team will select a plan that best suits their needs given their realities. These realities include the following:

- **We have fewer children**
  In the past, large families allowed for the possibility of three-generation households. Today, the average family is much smaller. Obviously,

that reduces our choices and can place a heavy responsibility on those with fewer adult children.

- **We had children when we were older**
  We married later than our parents did and were older when we had our children. Our children are likely to be in early adulthood when we retire. They may just be starting families and careers and may not be ready to assume responsibility for us.

- **Our children may live in other communities**
  For several generations, adult children have scattered to different parts of North America and the world to pursue careers and other opportunities. It is less likely that they will live in our community. This not only reduces our emotional connection with them, it also means that we can't count on as much support from them.

- **We have no children**
  It is equally important for people who have no children to actively recruit someone to fill the role of partner. As indicated earlier, this can be a relative or a younger friend. As with parents and adult children, meetings should occur regularly, and the partners we choose should be authorized to serve as our proxy.

- **We now live much longer**
  Because many of us can expect to live about twenty or more years after retirement, our partners may need to be involved with us for a much longer time. Although we can receive some

support from community agencies, someone needs to serve as the coordinator to ensure that our needs are being met. Generally our partners can do that best.

- **Some of us are divorced**
  Increasingly, seniors are divorced when they begin retirement. They may also have adult children who are divorced. Divorce can cause mixed loyalties, remarriages, and other issues. This disruption in family life can be overwhelming when it comes to planning for our senior years. Above all, it can cloud the parent–adult child relationship at the very time we need to be forming a new partnership with them.

- **Family conflict**
  Some of us are in families in which there is significant conflict. It may be between spouses, between parents and adult children, or even between the adult children. It is important to identify the issues and begin to find resolution to the differences. Conflict tends to intensify during a crisis, and if it is not resolved, it can lead to unfavorable outcomes for them and for us.

Beginning and continuing our conversations

Purposeful conversations between us and our partners in aging can be challenging, but they are necessary. Scheduled meetings can help all parties to develop common goals and create a plan that guides decision-making. Here are suggestions about how to get the conversations started:

- Seniors assume an attitude of humility and openness.
- Partners assume an attitude of sensitivity and patience.
- Either seniors or partners can take the lead in starting the conversations and then in setting up the meetings.
- Either seniors or partners can explain why the partnership is important and how it might work.
- Partners express their feelings about this new relationship, ask questions, talk about what they can offer, and reveal their areas of interest and skills.
- Discussions should include finances, housing needs, health, safety, and end-of-life wishes.
- It is helpful if someone takes minutes and then distributes copies to all participants.
- If it is adult children who are the partners and they live at a distance, meetings can be scheduled on holidays or vacations. Conference calls and video chats can also be helpful.
- The goal is to develop a plan that conveys the wishes and needs of the seniors and their partners. The plan should be updated as circumstances change.

Ending thoughts

As we enter our senior years, a partnership with our adult children or other partners assists us in preparing for our future. Failing to have these conversations can lead to decision-making in a crisis and to undesirable outcomes. Aging goes better when the people who are most directly involved have worked together to create a plan based on carefully considered choices. Let the partnerships begin!

Thinking and Planning Ahead

1. As an aging adult, what would keep you from forming a partnership with your adult children or a substitute partner?
2. Without this partnership, how do you anticipate facing the challenges that are ahead of you? Should we just hope that everything will work out on its own?
3. How can your partner be the most supportive to you?
4. As an adult child, relative, or close friend, when did you first recognize that your parents/aging partners were declining?
5. How will you adjust your life to accommodate the needs of those you serve?
6. How will you feel if your parents/partners resist you in creating a plan for their future?

The Conversation Within

DAD (to self): *Last month, the boss looked so happy at his retirement party. He talked about the traveling he and his wife were finally going to do. About how nice it would be when he could get tee time during the week when the golf courses aren't so crowded. But when I saw him at Rotary Club a month later, he admitted that he missed work—the socializing, the structure, and even the respect he felt when he was CEO. I was surprised that he talked so openly.*

I'm only a couple of years away from retirement. I've tried not to let work be my whole life, but I'm not big on hobbies. And I can't see myself pushing wheelchairs around the hospital. I know some men enjoy volunteering, but somehow it seems like busy work to me—something people do to keep from getting bored. After years of having a job that has been very satisfying, maybe I'll have the same experience as my boss when I retire. It might be best if I just keep working.

MOM (to self): *After thirty years of teaching, I'm ready for something else. The district has a good plan for teachers who retire early. I don't need the job. And every year the kids are harder to teach. It seems that half of my students are on medication for ADD. Parents aren't as supportive as they used to be. Now they just take the side of their child and blame the problems on teachers.*

Besides, our daughter could use some help with her children now that she has gone back to work. I felt bad when I couldn't help her before, when she really needed it. It will also be easier for me to visit Mom in the retirement community. She keeps calling me. I feel guilty when I can't go to see her as often as she wants.

UNMARRIED UNCLE (to self): *The big day is coming. It's hard to believe that I'll be retired next week. That means the end of stress and not having to put up with things I don't like to do. But, will I get lonely? I know that I can still get together with some of my friends from work, but will it be the same if we're not working together? And all of those trips my married friends take when they retire, I don't think I can do that alone. I have some family members I can turn to, but I can't depend on them to be my friends.*

We all carry on conversations with ourselves. Self-talk began when we were young children. We had animated discussions with imaginary playmates. During our teen years, some of us used diaries for this purpose. Adults don't speak with imaginary playmates, and most of us don't write in diaries, but we still talk to ourselves. In fact, self-talk is a vital way to process what is going on around us and within us.

We tend to guard our inner conversations closely. When we were very young, we stopped the chats with our imaginary friends when someone came into the room. We kept the secrets private during our teen years by hiding our diaries. Now, when we are asked what is on our minds, we get uncomfortable and often give general answers. As when we were younger, we still prefer keeping our inner thoughts to ourselves.

Concealing thoughts about aging

The wish to conceal private thoughts may increase as we enter our senior years. We may try to ignore these thoughts by jumping headlong into new activities, travel, and frenzy. But our life is changing and our future is unknown. Like it or not, our identity is being redefined, and our life purpose is in flux. We have much to ponder but little that we are ready to share with other people.

In part, we keep our thoughts—especially negative ones—to ourselves because we don't want to worry others who might think they have to solve our problems. Mostly, though, we hide these thoughts because we are protecting a side of ourselves that we aren't ready to have others see. That side contains our fears, self-doubts, disappointments, and our anger. We do, after all, have an image to maintain, and showing our emotions might reveal something that we want to keep private. We may even keep these thoughts from those closest to us.

The emotional part of our inner conversation may be the hardest to talk about. How do we explain feeling less valued since retirement? We aren't included in important meetings, the phone calls stop coming, and emails have all but disappeared. We wonder why friends from work no longer ask us to go out to lunch. At the same time, we discover that lifting the bag of salt for the water softener is more of a challenge, and opening jar lids is harder. Perhaps the biggest concern is that we are thinking about entering our last life stage, something that none of us can fully prepare for.

Wondering about the thoughts of our partners

While we are pondering our own thoughts about aging, we wonder what our adult children or our partners are thinking. Because we are still in good health and adjusting well to retirement, we hope that we aren't on their mind much. After all, they're busy and have their own things to think about. In some ways, we don't feel ready to talk because there are some pretty unpleasant things to discuss, and it seems easier to postpone the conversations for another day. We'll start the conversations when we have to. Then we'll figure out what we have to.

Anticipating retirement

In the years leading up to retirement, we think positively about the future. We look forward to no longer carrying as much responsibility. We anticipate being our own bosses and determining how we spend our time. We hear about the new ways we as seniors can contribute to society and of the good things that can happen during retirement, including spending more time with our grandchildren and friends. Some of us create a to-do list of unfinished projects that we can finally get to. We promise ourselves that we will work on getting our bodies in shape. Others of us dream about buying an RV for a long trip across the country.

In a weaker moment, some "what if" scenarios slip into our minds. What if we don't have enough money and need to delay retirement? What if we get bored? What if we miss our friends at work? If we are married, we might wonder whether we will get on our spouse's nerves. Not far from our minds is the thought of having medical crises, like a heart attack, or developing dementia. We may notice that we are having trouble climbing steps or are forgetting where we put our keys. But we usually don't entertain these thoughts very long. We are on a countdown to freedom.

Life after the retirement party

On our last day at work, we turn in our keys, clean off our desks, or punch out at the time clock for the last time. We close the book on a lifetime of work. Some of us will be honored at a retirement party, while others will be given best wishes as we go out the door. They tell us how much they'll miss us and promise to stay in touch. With mixed feelings, we know that an important life stage has come to an end.

We are now a former teacher, nurse, business owner, salesperson, hairdresser, trucker, or whatever our career was. When we meet people, that identity is no longer a part of us. Saying that we are retired doesn't carry much weight. This lack of identity can make conversations awkward. In the past, our careers opened doors socially, gave us respect, and carried a kind of pedigree. What we did was who we were. It is difficult for us to think of ourselves in any other way. We can tell people what we *used* to do, but that doesn't have much relevance anymore.

The loss of identity, though, is only a part of what we miss. We leave behind important friendships and social networks. Even though many of us counted down the days until we could retire, we were surprised at how empty we felt when it finally came. There was a real vacuum from not having a schedule or a routine. The structure from our jobs helped shape our lives for many years, and now it is gone.

Perhaps most important is that these changes signal that our life is more about *endings* than it is about *beginnings*. The days of growing and expanding are over. Now it is about a death of both *doing* and *being*. Dying is not just a physical event. It very much involves the dying of the self. For some of us, that is gradual, and for others, sudden. Ultimately, it causes many of us to lose our passion for continuing. Surely that happens in stages, and certainly more quickly when our health declines.

When we visit a nursing care facility and see residents going through an entire meal without saying a word or slumped over in a wheelchair, these losses become more real. Some of them simply appear to have given up. Maybe it is because their health has declined. Perhaps they are tired of playing Bingo or putting puzzles together. Has life for these persons already ended? Is that what we have to look forward to?

Thinking about the alternatives

One of our friends talks about the joy she feels when she reads stories to children at the library since her retirement. And another who is active on the board of the local food bank. At the same time, we read in the paper about seniors who audit courses at the local community college and others who serve as guides at the museum.

Many of the people we meet describe the present time as the best part of their lives. We are encouraged when we hear that emotional health—even physical health—can be improved by the choices we make. What is somewhat sobering, however, is that, if we found life to be challenging earlier, it may be even more so now. But it doesn't have to be that way. We can choose to find purpose and hope even in this stage of our life. It will only come if we make that choice, though.

Beginning the journey: The first steps

After the last sip of coffee with friends at a restaurant, we return to a house that seems strangely empty. It used to be the refuge to which we returned after long hours of work. It was a special place to recover from the wounds of battle. Now it is silent and somehow less welcoming. In the midst of our new freedom, we have a feeling that something is missing.

But the house hasn't changed at all; it isn't really empty. Maybe the emptiness is within us. The void can't completely be filled by golf and breakfasts with friends. Yes, the trip to Hawaii was wonderful, but the memories wore off quickly. We know we can't find contentment just through traveling. We may even tire of the projects that we set up for ourselves. We had been eager to get started on them, but now we wonder why we have lost interest. Maybe it's because we've built too many birdhouses or knitted more afghans than we have use for.

Physical changes

Much as we may try to ignore it, our bodies are showing signs of aging. Every day, it seems we sag a little more. We've given up trying to shed the extra pounds. Our hair is thinner, and we may stop trying to hide the gray. We begin to notice that we are less steady on our feet and have trouble reaching our toes to cut our nails. It's a challenge to hear conversations in a noisy room. At class reunions, we feel discouraged when old friends aren't quite sure who we are. If at one time we felt attractive, we feel less so now. Having others tell us that we have a pleasing personality may be well intentioned, but it somehow feels patronizing. And we feel somewhat irritated when people tell us how good we look "for your age."

It worries us that we take daily medications to control cholesterol and blood pressure. Pillboxes are for old people. We experience more pain and find it a challenge to play competitive sports. We tire more quickly. It's common to nod off in the evenings while reading or watching TV.

Most of the time, we are able to convince ourselves that these things are mere annoyances. It could be worse. When we are with our friends, our common laments help create a spirit of camaraderie. Increasingly, we share inner thoughts as we compare health-status reports. We use humor as an attempt to rub salve on our emotional wounds. For now, we try not to complain because much of life is going well. Our thoughts of uncertainty are minimal and they remain unspoken.

Dependency and death

And then we begin to hear about peers who died suddenly and others who are diagnosed with cancer. We have known for some time that our college roommate is in a nursing home with ALS. When attending funerals, we think we see fear in the eyes of our peers. For the first time in our lives, we can't escape the images of disability and even death. Perhaps most troubling of all, we fear becoming dependent on others. Being self-reliant is deeply ingrained in how we see ourselves.

Those of us who are married occasionally consider what it would be like if our spouse died. We imagine enormous feelings of emptiness and grief. Could we survive financially? Could we cope day to day? It is hard to think of remarrying because of loyalty to our spouse. What would it mean to our children and grandchildren if one of us died? We don't want to dwell too long on these realities.

Search for peace

All of our concerns, though, seem far away in the early retirement years. When we think clearly, we know the numbers are on our side. Our parents lived well into their eighties, and the doctor tells us we're in good shape. We push our worst-case scenarios off for another time. We must seize the day. There is much to live for. We enjoy new activities and deeper friendships now that we have more time. It's reassuring.

We feel lucky to live in a community where lots of cultural programs are available. Most offer senior discounts. A senior center in our neighborhood has a monthly gathering for people our age. We're finding a new life. We're becoming somebody different than we were. Aging is not so bad. In some ways, it's better because we're not tied down with expectations. We're not competing. Maybe we're discovering what just *being* means. We know that it's better than *not* being.

Perhaps most helpful is that we learn to accept—even embrace—the fact that life and death are normal at this stage. We can treasure the moment and all the love and attention that are given to us. We don't have to *do* anything anymore. No more performances or putting on our best face.

The *being* that matters doesn't get measured or evaluated. We are valued and our life—and death—are a part of a sacred cycle. We are beginning to find peace.

Ending thoughts

All of us have inner conversations. They help guide us through lives that are complicated and always changing. It is through these inner conversations that we discover our feelings and map out plans for important choices. Up to a point, it is important that our conversations are kept private because, if we said everything on our mind, we might not have many friends, and we could say things we would later regret.

Throughout our lives, it has been important for us to share some of our internal conversations with others. It is a way of testing our views to see if they are valid. Many times we make midcourse corrections based on the feedback we receive. When we are open with the people who matter to us, we often get affirmation and encouragement that strengthens us.

As we enter our senior years, it is more important than ever that we bring our inner conversations out into the open. We've never been in this stage before. Most importantly, this stage is about losses, the unknown, and the surrender of self. Not since childhood will we need so much care from others. We must turn to our adult children or to family and friends to become our partners throughout this time. We no longer need to protect them from the realities that we are all facing—we are in this journey together. The journey can only be successful when we engage in open and repeated conversations with each other. While we may continue to have our private thoughts, it is very important that the most urgent concerns be shared with those who walk with us. Only then can we face the end with courage and achieve the peace we all seek.

Thinking and Planning Ahead

1. Keep a journal and review it monthly with your partners.

2. Practice talking openly with your spouse or trusted friend.

3. Use birthdays as a special time to reflect and anticipate the future.

4. Continue to discuss your biggest concerns, and use your partners to find solutions.

5. Seek new ways to discover and express joy and hope.

6. What is your biggest worry when you think about your future?

7. If you haven't shared that worry with anyone, why not?

8. What gives you purpose now?

9. Is just "being" enough for you? Why? Why not?

10. What "doing" gives you satisfaction?

Marital Conversations

WIFE: *I'm starting to worry about how much you're just sitting around watching TV—especially sports. You keep saying that you deserve a break, but it's been a few months now. You know the yard needs mowing, and our son could use some help with the deck he's building. And I'm bothered by your grumpiness. I thought we were both looking forward to retirement. We had lots of dreams. It has to be better than this.*

HUSBAND: *I still can't figure out where you get all your energy. You're running all over the place, going to committee meetings at the library, and being over at our daughter's. I thought when we retired we'd take it easy. Maybe you're right about the TV. I know the yard needs to be mowed, and I'll call our son to see if he needs help. But it's hard not to have any schedule now. Before, every day of my life was planned. Now, every day is a big blank. I still can't figure out why it all seems so easy for you.*

After years of looking forward to retirement, we have both finally arrived. Freedom from the demands of work feels good. Our loyalties are no longer divided. The marriage doesn't have to take second place to work, and our focus can now be on each other. The phone doesn't ring with requests to come in to work early or to make one more trip for the company. Neither of us has a distracted look as we sit across the breakfast table from each other. Perhaps the greatest gift of retirement is that we don't have to set the alarm clock anymore.

We have been planning a long time for a trip to celebrate this milestone. But now it is behind us. We saw some wonderful scenery and had lots of uninterrupted time to talk. It gave us an opportunity to get to know each other in a new way. Returning home and establishing new routines also feels good. We have to admit that living out of a suitcase and having no schedule was getting old.

For some of us, these celebration excursions can bring out differences. Maybe it is the lack of structure that creates the stress. Partway into their travel, Daryl and Lila wished they had planned better for their time together. Daryl was eager to get started because he had been retired several years and was biding his time until Lila retired. They sold their home, purchased a motor home, and planned a trip with flexible destinations and few deadlines. But, they soon found themselves directionless and in tension with each other. Lila missed the satisfaction that she got from her work and felt uncomfortable with not having a home to return to. Daryl, however, was enjoying the adventure and the freedom of not having to follow a schedule.

In the midst of their frustrations they made a wonderful discovery when they visited an art gallery. While there, Lila realized she would like to develop a framing business as a part of her work as an artist. After leaving the gallery, they decided to return to learn more about the framing business. During the rest of the trip, they spent many good hours planning for the new business. Soon after their trip ended, they bought a house that could be adapted for Lila's new studio. That discovery has been important to both of them in the years since then.

No preparation

When we enter retirement, many of us aren't prepared for the changes that will happen in our marriages. Although we may have sought advice about finances and other things before we retired, few of us thought about how retirement could affect our relationship. In fact, the glossy brochures that we received showing retired couples smiling, embracing, or engaging in invigorating activities made it all look very inviting. Nowhere did we read about the adjustments that we would need to make. None of us got an orientation to retirement.

That is ironic considering the fact that, throughout our lifetime, we were given orientations to virtually every change that came along. It all began with kindergarten and continued through the time we enrolled in college. We also received orientations to new jobs, had premarital counseling, birthing classes, and parenting classes. Now, during this important transition, we are left to make the adjustment on our own.

More years together

Perhaps an orientation to retirement hasn't been a priority because, several generations ago, people didn't live nearly as long, and comparatively few retired. In the early 1900s, my (Marlene's) maternal grandmother died at the age of twenty-eight and my paternal grandfather died when he was twenty-three, so they and their spouses never experienced retirement together. The first broad-scale recognition of retirement in the United States didn't take place until 1935, when the Social Security program was created.[1] For the first time in this country, persons who lived to age sixty-five could retire because they received a pension. Longevity has increased since then, and most of us expect to live many more years after retirement. Fiftieth wedding anniversary celebrations are now commonplace.

While this opportunity to be together for a longer time is a wonderful gift, it is not without its challenges, including an increase in conflict. It may be because we have extra time on our hands, changes in roles, or a loss of identity. These changes make it necessary to find new ways to relate to each other.

To add to our burden are the expectations of marriage that come from popular culture. In recent years, we have been flooded with advice about the need to understand ourselves better, achieve interpersonal compatibility, improve sexual techniques, develop better communication skills, and to learn how to handle conflict. Perhaps most challenging of all is that there is an expectation to be *soulmates*. During retirement, all of these can be magnified by the extra time we spend together.

Ordinary time together

Fortunately, for most of us, what *brought* us together is what *keeps* us together. Even though the physical attraction is different now than when we first met, the positive characteristics we saw in each other are still there—humor, warmth, compassion, energy, and stability. Some of us have been strengthened by our beliefs and values. Some by supporting each other during stressful times like a child's illness, death of friends, financial challenges, and other stresses. At the same time, the successes we experienced over the years are a source of celebration.

What may have strengthened us most were the ordinary moments—the cuddling, back rubs, the sharing of chores, long trips to visit the children in college, and the many times when nothing in particular was happening. As in the past, most of the time now is spent doing ordinary things—talking about the weather, what to have for dinner, the grandchildren, events in the neighborhood, and watching our favorite TV show. These chats are the foundation of marriage at all ages. Beyond keeping us informed, they keep us connected. Now, in retirement, we depend on the ordinary moments even more. We accept every day as a gift knowing that we can't take each other for granted.

Settling unresolved differences

Although all of us experience some conflict in marriage, it is usually minor, and we tend to ignore it. However, some differences—whether from the past or the present—can cause deep hurts, and we should seek resolution from a skilled third party while we are still able to do so. It is important that we grant each other forgiveness and find new ways of relating to each other—even at this stage of our lives. We shouldn't wait for another day because that day may never come. Too many marriages have ended with the sudden death of a spouse before the couple could forgive and reconcile, leaving the survivors with feelings that are hard to resolve.

To help avoid living with regrets, Peter and Elfrieda Dyck made a commitment early in their marriage to practice forgiveness daily. Before going to sleep, they would utter the phrase *nichts zwischen uns* in their native German language, meaning that there are no unresolved differences between them. They kept that promise throughout more than fifty years of marriage. When Elfrieda died, Peter had a sense of peace, knowing that nothing was left unresolved.

It is also vital that we work out our differences for the sake of our adult children. Jim and Sue recognized that there were some ongoing issues between them, and they sought marriage counseling. As a part of their healing, they invited their adult children to a weekend gathering at a retreat center. There they asked forgiveness for the impact that their conflict had on the children during their growing-up years. The children were touched by their openness and granted forgiveness. They shared tears of joy. The whole family celebrated together in a new way. This set the stage for having the adult children join them as partners in planning for the many changes that were to come as the parents began to decline.

Shared responsibilities

In our pre-retirement years, many of us developed rather distinctive marital roles that were shaped by career demands, schedules, and by our preferences and abilities. For the sake of efficiency, the responsibilities that we accepted at home tended to follow a predictable pattern: wives did the cooking, husbands did the yard work. In retirement, we realize that the tasks we performed before may need to change—in part because of fairness and in part because of necessity. We may even go through a period of uncertainty about our new responsibilities. Making these changes can be difficult.

Many of us negotiate our way through these changes. Willingness to learn new skills strengthens our relationship and prepares us for the time when one of us declines in health or dies. Both of us should learn the life skills needed for daily living. It is important to start the conversations about these changes early in our retirement.

Conversations about free time

In the early years of retirement, many of us have trouble knowing how to spend our free time. Some put energy into neglected work around the house. Others clean out any spare rooms and get rid of things that are no longer needed. After those tasks are finished, many of us don't know what to do next. When there are no particular schedules or demands, we can lose focus. Our motivation sags, and we can sink into apathy. We may find it difficult to get started on projects or to complete those we began. This time of uncertainty can lead to pointless arguments.

We may find enjoyment from having part-time work or from volunteering. Others develop hobbies or take up some form of recreation. While we do many of these activities individually, we can find it satisfying to do new things together, such as gardening, cooking, playing tennis, or hosting. Some of us simply begin walking together—a form of exercise that is cheap, requires no skill, is good for our health, and can provide a time of uninterrupted discussion.

One of the most important ways we can find meaning is by expanding the time we spend with friends. Although they were important to us before, we need them now more than ever. They are a valuable source of love and support and can bring a freshness that we need to keep our relation-ship from becoming stale. Some prefer their time with other couples to include playing table games, going to concerts, or other kinds of activity. Most just enjoy the time chatting, lamenting, and laughing.

Conversations about health and caregiving

One of the most urgent conversations between spouses is about health. Many of us avoid talking about it because we are in good health at the moment. Others of us avoid the subject because we aren't ready to face our decline and death. It is common to ignore changes in each other's health long after others see them. The changes may be as minor as hearing loss or as major as a life-threatening condition.

It is important to have these talks because some ill-nesses can be resolved or minimized by early treatment. Even when the illness cannot be cured, it is important to deal with the realities of the present condition and to pre-pare for what is coming. Unfortunately, it is common to put off talking about health until we are forced to. Then, when one spouse is incapacitated and can no longer speak for themselves, the other spouse is left to make difficult deci-sions alone.

Another part of the discussion is about the caregiving that we may need to provide each other at some point. Some studies show that 88 percent of us will give significant care to our ailing spouse for an extended time.[2] The Rosalyn Carter Institute estimates that, because of this stress, one-third of caregivers will experience a decline in health and will age prematurely.[3] Providing this care can cause sleep deprivation, immune system deficiency, depression, chronic anxiety, loss of concentration, and premature death. It is important to talk about and prepare an alternate plan for caregiving.

Joy remembers when she realized that something was happening to her husband, Jim. They were returning from a trip to see an adult child, and Jim couldn't find their car in the airport parking lot. After some time riding around with a very patient shuttle driver, they located the car. Jim then jumped out of the shuttle, ran to the car, and drove off without Joy or their luggage. Eventually they found each other, and Joy offered to drive home. Jim refused and made a number of wrong turns on the way. Joy knew then that her life would never be the same.

When she shared this experience with their children and family doctor, they all thought she was making too much of it, suggesting that Jim was just fatigued. But his disorientation increased, and eventually Jim was diagnosed with Alzheimer's disease. It was not easy for Joy to assume responsibility for their finances and to make the decisions about the future of Jim's business. But it was important for her to do what she could to preserve Jim's dignity. As Jim lost more of his cognitive abilities and became increasingly confused, Joy wrote things on cards, such as "cut toenails," "I am Joy," "sit," "eat dinner," and so forth. The printed words seemed more comforting to him than spoken words. Clearly, what was being communicated was her love.

Lester's parents still lived alone in their old, two-story farmhouse when they were in their nineties. Family members became concerned that the parents weren't caring properly for each other. But when the family talked about help with day-to-day responsibilities, the mother insisted that she could take care of things by herself. Eventually, at the persistence of the family, they agreed to have someone come to help with bathing and meals. In spite of that, Lester's mother got up at four a.m., bathed herself and her husband, and prepared breakfast before the caregiver arrived. She and her husband were sitting in their favorite chairs, waiting, when the worker knocked on the door at seven a.m. It took a medical crisis to convince the parents that they were no longer able to provide adequate care for each other.

Conversations about finances

In our middle years, many of us begin planning for what our financial needs will be during retirement. We estimate our monthly benefits from Social Security, pensions, other sources of income, and at the same time, try to anticipate our expenses. Many of us consult with financial advisors to help make the best plan. Now in retirement, the planning we have done becomes relevant.

Unfortunately, many of us have disagreements with each other about finances. Sometimes it is because we approach saving and spending differently. In spite of these differences, the day-to-day management of finances is usually assumed by one of us. That includes paying the bills and doing the banking. It is important, though, for both of us to have a working knowledge of the finances to prevent surprises later on. This is vital for couples at all income levels. Working together on finances can lead to better decisions.

Conversations about housing

When we retire, most of us will be in the house where we've lived for many years. We are familiar with it, comfortable with the neighborhood, and have good memories there. In many ways, it has been a sacred space for us. But its size, layout, and features were set up for different circumstances, especially to provide for the needs of children. Now we may prefer more appropriate housing.

Talking about moving can be a difficult conversation. Our home can have a unique meaning for each of us, and we may be at different points regarding our wishes. We may want freedom from the care of the property or from cleaning rooms we no longer use. Apartments, condominiums, gated communities for people over fifty-five, and retirement communities with attached nursing facilities begin to look appealing.

But we may not be ready to downsize because we are still enjoying hosting friends, having family dinners, and wanting a place for the grandchildren to play. We may even stay where we are because we enjoy doing lawn care, gardening, or minor maintenance projects. We also hesitate to move because it is complicated and disruptive. We will need to get rid of some of our furniture, clean out the attic, and change addresses, among other things. If we are in disagreement about moving, the whole process is even more difficult.

Knowing *when* to move is perhaps the hardest part of the decision. Many people wait until circumstances force them to do so. Then one spouse has to make the decision alone. After Jean had a stroke and was moved to a long-term care facility, John sold their home and moved in with their daughter. Jean now cries about losing her home and not having been a part of the decision. They should have had the discussion earlier.

Companions to the end

As we enter retirement, many of us reflect with some satisfaction on the good memories from the years we have spent together. We may also have some regrets for our failures. But, we aren't ready to take a seat on the proverbial rocking chair or resign to a life of insignificance. We can still make strong contributions to our family, friends, and community. Making new discoveries that keep our marriage fresh is still possible.

At our wedding, most of us made sacred promises to each other. They have been the ballast in our boat that has kept it from tipping over. Hopefully, our commitment has served as an example to our children, friends, and to the broader community.

We become increasingly aware of our promise to stand by each other in sickness and in health. We know that we are on a decline that will lead to death. We are knit together on a journey that is painful but unavoidable. As our bodies begin to fail, the stronger spouse supports the weaker. When our minds fail, the one with greater awareness is a source of reality to the other.

Although our adult children can be a vital support during this time, most of us will be first responders for each other until the end. We do that even if our spouse is living in a nursing facility and may not be aware we are there. Our marriage has been a journey. As long as we can, we want to remain beside each other. We have a sacred companionship.

Ending thoughts

Though we may have been married for a long time, none of us has had a "senior" marriage. Now, we face circumstances that we haven't had to deal with before. Until now, our marriage has been focused on our children, our careers, finances, and maintaining a lifestyle. Even though we had many good moments with each other, our focus was often elsewhere.

Now, in many ways, it is just us. We are no longer onward and upward people. As we refocus on each other, we will need to discover new identities, new purpose, and a new use for our time and abilities. We will want to show each other special grace during this time of transition and uncertainty. We see each day as a gift. We won't take each other for granted and will anticipate the time when we need to care for each other. On this journey, we are knit together in ways we couldn't have been in our earlier years. We are beginning to broaden our understanding of intimacy.

Thinking and Planning Ahead

1. Set aside time to talk about how retirement and aging are affecting your relationship.

2. Explore new activities and friendships that can enrich your time together.

3. Discuss how much time to spend together and how much to spend apart.

4. Expand daily expressions of gratitude and support.

5. What keeps you from talking about the changes that will come?

6. How has retirement affected you and your spouse differently?

7. What new skills are important for each spouse to develop?

8. How can we resolve differences between us?

The Voice of the Caregiver: Adult Children and Others

DAUGHTER: *Did you know that Jim's parents moved to a nursing home? They're just a little bit older than Mom and Dad. I'm not ready to see our parents surrounded by old people and unable to care for themselves anymore. Can you imagine seeing them getting on the home's bus to take them to a concert? Or playing cards to pass the time? But I do think about what would happen if one of them got sick— maybe had a stroke. I know I couldn't take care of them. I'm plenty busy with my job and running our three kids around.*

SON: *It does seem like our relationship with them is changing. Right now, I don't feel responsible for them, but I know it won't stay that way. That's probably why they've invited* *us to a family meeting. They said it is about what our rela-tionship with them should be as they get older—especially about their finances, their health, and where they should live in the future. They even want to talk about the papers they signed to not keep them on respirators and IVs when they're near death. But I don't know if I'm ready for this. It feels too much like switching roles.*

NIECE: *Aunt Lily just called and asked me if I could go with her to the doctor. She hasn't felt well lately and isn't sure she will be able to remember what the doctor tells her if she goes by herself. I am concerned about her dizziness and confusion, and I know her daughter, Marge, can't fly in from California just for this. But I do wonder if she might feel I'm intruding. I'm plenty busy now, but somebody should go with her. Besides, Lily's always been special to me.*

FRIEND: *My golfing buddy, Ben, surprised me when he approached me about helping him to make decisions about his finances. I feel a bit awkward stepping into this role because I'm twenty years younger, but I do know that he has made some bad choices with his money lately. It must be hard for him, especially now that he lost his wife and has no children. I read in the paper about all the elderly people being scammed, so maybe I should agree to help him.*

Caring for seniors can be performed in many ways and by a variety of persons. The longer people live, the more they will need support from others. For the most part, we, as caregivers, assume the role of coordinating their care and attending to their needs in a number of important ways. Most of us will not give physical care such as bathing. And medical care is usually performed by professionals. Our role, however, is very critical. It is important for us to begin meeting with them early in their senior years to estab- lish trust and to determine together what their needs are. We will also define our role and become acquainted with their finances, health, housing, and personal and emotional needs. We then develop a plan together to ensure that their needs will be addressed. Perhaps just as important is that we are choosing to become their partners during these years.

As caregivers, some of us will be their sons or daughters. Others of us will be nieces, nephews, siblings, or trusted friends. What's most important is that no senior should go through this challenging life stage alone; rather, everyone should be attended by a younger, caring, and competent person. Because of their diminishing abilities, seniors are faced with too many risks.

It can be hard for us adult children to see our parents decline, becoming forgetful, weak, and diminished. Until now, the thought of them needing help from us rarely crossed our minds because they have been active, healthy, and self-reliant. It seems like only yesterday that they were babysitting our children, helping us with home repairs, offering advice about finances, and other things.

Those of us who are caregivers to aunts, uncles, and friends may feel less comfortable in our role because we aren't their offspring. Because of that, some of us may accept our assignment with some hesitation, wondering if we have a right to make decisions for them or to be firm when changes are needed in the plan. On the other hand, we aren't quite as burdened by the emotions that adult children often are, and perhaps we can be more objective.

Some of us may be asked to provide care for several seniors at the same time. Sometimes it includes both parents. Indeed, some studies show that approximately 30 percent of us will care for two or more persons!

Lucy experienced that situation when she served as her parents' caregiver during the last years of their lives while also offering care for two of her aunts. Even though one aunt is now living in a continuing care facility, Lucy is in contact with her on a regular basis and supports her in other ways. Her other aunt lives in her own home at age ninety-three with her deaf son. Lucy is pleased to accompany her to doctor appointments. A son who lives in Florida offers some support, but relies on Lucy for more immediate care for his mother. Unexpectedly, Lucy's single brother had a medical crisis and also needed support. In addition to this caregiving, she is active with her children and grandchildren and is committed to preserving time for her marriage—and for herself.

When we have siblings, it is important to involve them in providing some of the care for our parents. To ensure that the best care plan is put in place, it is important that we meet together as a family when our parents approach their senior years. Meetings—including our parents—will continue at regular intervals afterward and will be supplemented by regular phone and email updates. What is most helpful is for the family to become a team, each with separate tasks and that the family forms a close relationship with the senior's other caregivers, including the physician, lawyer, financial advisor, and other professionals. The same process can be helpful when we are the caregiver for aunts, uncles, or friends.

Julie and her siblings started to have monthly lunches together some years ago as a way of staying in touch with each other about the needs of their parents. When her brother who lived out of town wasn't able to join them, someone would update him and invite his feedback. As their parents' health began to fail, the siblings were better prepared to work together. To make things easier, one of the grandchildren prepared a spread sheet outlining visitation and task assignments for everyone involved.

Forming this team is important because some studies show that at least 40 percent of us will give care to our parents at some point. Typically, daughters provide more personal care and home management assistance while sons tend to help with legal and financial matters. We are, on average, forty-six years old when the caregiving begins.[1] Many of us still have at least one child at home, and about half of us are working full-time while simultaneously offering twenty-four hours of unpaid care to our parent. Interestingly, our involvement with an aging parent often comes at about the same time that we are anticipating becoming empty nesters. In some cases, that caregiving role may come even sooner: The National Alliance for Caregivers reported in 2015 that 20 percent of caregivers are eighteen to thirty-four years of age. Obviously, this can have a significant impact on the careers and relationships of people at that age as well.

Those of us who are caregivers for aunts, uncles, and friends may also be involved in demanding careers, juggling children's schedules, and relating to a spouse. If we are single, we might have careers that are important as well as active friendships. Whatever our circumstances, we may find it challenging to set aside time and energy for these various responsibilities.

David was faced with this reality. He and his wife, Karen, were fully focused on parenting their nineteen-year-old daughter and their fourteen-year-old son when they learned that his father was having leg pain and was being evaluated by several doctors. Sometime later when he went to visit his father, David found it hard to see the man who was once so strong and healthy now sitting in a wheelchair. It was even harder when he learned that his father was diagnosed with cancer.

Over the next seven months, David accepted his role as caregiver. He occasionally set aside work and family responsibilities to drive seven hours to be with his father when he was receiving treatment. Karen made the trip on alternate weeks to support her mother-in-law. Following his father's death, David and Karen made additional trips to comfort David's mother and to help her plan for the future.

Maureen had been a sensitive person from early childhood and, after graduating from high school, chose to become a nurse. That sensitivity made her aware of the needs of her parents even before they were seniors. Nevertheless, she was not prepared to begin the caregiving role when her father had a heart attack at age fifty-two. She was twenty-five at that time and had two sons, ages two and four. She remembers asking an aunt, "How will I be able to give care to my father, my young children, and also continue my work as a nurse?" "You just have to do it," the aunt replied.

Over the next eight years, Maureen was her parents' primary on-call responder and caregiver. She got some help from a sister when she visited from out of state. In reflecting back on the care she gave her parents, Maureen has no regrets and would do it again. She and her husband, Al, a caregiver to his own parents, became even more patient, compassionate, and forgiving through their experiences. They see the model they established with their parents now reflected in the ways their sons relate to them.

The importance of conversations

Caregiving is more challenging today because more of us come from small families and have moved away from our home communities, making it harder to share tasks and coordinate with local services for our aging parents, relatives, and friends. Thus it is especially important that we meet early in our parents' retirement years to talk about how we will share the responsibilities. Too often the sibling who lives closest or is single is expected to do more. That can feel unfair and lead to resentment. It is vital to engage other persons to share the load and to secure services that are available in the community. This is even more important if we have no siblings.

Mary stayed near home and assumed a great deal of responsibility for her parents. She had many siblings, but most of them had moved away. She took leadership in scheduling a family meeting to talk about sharing the responsibilities. As a result, one sibling volunteered to be executor, one to handle the parents' finances, and one to do research on the kind of services available in their parents' community. The siblings who lived closer offered more hands-on care. They checked in with each other regularly about gaps in the care plan.

Kristen was in her thirties when she began to talk with her retired parents about moving from their home in Oregon to her community in Pennsylvania. She wanted them to be able to enjoy her children as they were growing up and to have her parents' support during this demanding time of her life. Kristen also knew that if they stayed in Oregon, she couldn't be much help to them as they aged.

In the eight years since they moved, the benefits have been greater than anyone expected. Kristen has the satisfaction of seeing her parents interact with her children, attend some of their activities at school and church, and babysit when she and her husband, Johncey, need a night off.

Since the move, Kristen and her parents have had medical problems that required surgery. Being in the same community has made it possible for them to care for each other. Most of all, a system of support is now in place for the future.

Fortunately, most of us can develop a plan to meet our parents' needs. Typically, one sibling emerges as a leader and the primary caregiver. The other siblings are supportive of that person and offer assistance when possible. However, if siblings don't offer that help, the primary caregiver should request it—sometimes for specific tasks, as well as asking for time off. It's important for the leader to communicate regularly to the siblings to inform them about any changes that are happening with the parents in order to keep them engaged in decision-making.

Family conflict

Caregivers are presented with special challenges today because people live longer and are often in declining health. The seniors may not adjust well to their losses and the role changes that are happening. They may become more secretive about finances and resist taking suggestions about health, driving, and house maintenance well. Losing their independence is hard and can make them resistant to shared decision-making.

Sometimes we, the caregivers, are responsible for creating conflict. Some of us might still be angry about the way our parents treated us when we were young. Perhaps they were emotionally distant, gave us little support, or were even abusive. Maybe they were too busy with their careers. Now we find it difficult to show compassion to them and can even resent the fact that we are expected to give them care. On the other hand, we may have trouble caring for them because we have been too dependent on them throughout our lives, and now we can't switch roles when they need help from us.

Some of us, though, had good relationships with our parents yet are so deeply engaged in our careers and activities that we are unwilling to become a part of their care team. We depend on the services that are available in the community to meet their needs. Though we are not in conflict with them, we are not engaged either.

Making a care plan is difficult when some siblings choose to not get involved or disagree about what should be done for parents. These responses may be a continuation of the patterns that started during our childhood. Some of us were favored by parents while others felt rejected. Levels of attachment to each other and to our parents varied. Changes are hard to make in our relationships now because we are all experiencing heightened emotions from seeing our parents declining.

Finding solutions

It is so important that we find new ways of relating to each other because the failure to do so will be hurtful to all of us. Conflict can alienate us from our siblings and present a negative model to our children. But it doesn't have to be that way. We can choose to set aside past patterns and become effective partners as we work together.

That will happen more effectively if we focus on the needs of our parents and not our own. Doing so can help us have more productive family meetings. Some of these meet-ings can be limited to siblings, and some can include par-ents. It is important to keep the focus on their immediate needs while, at the same time, trying to anticipate future needs. Throughout the process, it is important that we share feelings openly and listen to each other with respect.

However, some families are unable to make these changes on their own and need the mediation of a coun-selor. If a sibling or either of the parents refuse to meet, it is important that the rest of the family move ahead with counseling to develop and implement the plan of care.

Those of us who are a caregiver to a senior who is not our parent might also find the aging relative or friend resis-tant to our ideas. In addition, they may be a part of an extended family that either has negative feelings toward them or us. There, too, we should seek the help of a coun-selor. Failing to do so often leads to hurtful outcomes for everyone, perhaps conflicting over the settling of a will.

Other complications

The care plan is also made more difficult if our parents are divorced. We can be caught between them when they are at odds with each other. If we view one parent as "at fault" and the other as the "victim," we can find it hard to know how to reach out to the "at-fault" parent. We may reject that parent because of what s/he "did to all of us." On the other hand, we may need to guard against overprotecting the parent we see as the victim. If we ourselves are divorced, the situation can become even more challenging.

If our parents remarry after a divorce, or even after the death of their spouse, our caregiving often becomes more complicated. Sometimes a stepparent can see us as an intruder or may identify us with the other parent. The love that we feel for our parent can be clouded by the ambivalence that we feel toward their new spouse. Our loyalties can be divided and confusing.

We might feel awkward about our caregiving role—especially when the stepparent begins to decline and needs assistance. It is common for stepchildren to be unclear about what their relationship should be with their stepparent and stepsiblings. Some feel that they have no role in the plan of care. The importance of open and ongoing conversations cannot be stressed enough.

Finding forgiveness

If we have experienced any of these painful circumstances, we may need to take the first step to make peace. As long as our parents are in good health, there is still time to talk, allowing hurts to be shared and resolved. It may not happen immediately, but when it does, the family can move forward with a spirit of peace.

For some of us, it may not be necessary to go back over wounds from the past or to expect complete healing to take place. In fact, reopening old wounds may create some new complications that may be just as divisive. What is important is that we create an attitude of forgiveness, even if full reconciliation hasn't taken place. We all live with some degree of disharmony and imperfection in relationships—even in the best of circumstances.

As Amy sat by her mother's bedside in the last year of her life, she decided to forgive her for the emotional abuse she had experienced from her mother over the years. Amy took that step even though her mother hadn't asked for it. When she realized that her mother didn't even know how hurtful she had been, Amy began to feel some compassion and was able to say she loved her. To Amy's great surprise, her mother said, "I love you too!"—something Amy had never heard growing up. After her mother died, Amy felt no more resentment and is now at peace.

Forgiving parents is not easy. We must set aside past hurts and accept who they are today. We need to believe that our parents did the best they could in their circumstances. As parents ourselves now, we too make mistakes and will need our children's forgiveness. When we demonstrate a forgiving spirit, we offer a wonderful model for our children and grandchildren.

In a similar way, if we have conflict with our siblings, it is helpful to make peace with them while our parents are alive. Here, too, it may be helpful to seek the services of a counselor to bring about reconciliation. It is more difficult to accomplish that after our parent's death.

That happened with Les, who was estranged from his siblings for most of his adult life. His family rarely got together, and when they did, the brothers never talked. When Les died unexpectedly in his early sixties, a brother who attended the funeral was emotionally moved by the tributes he heard about Les. That allowed him to set aside his anger. He expressed regret that he and Les hadn't reconciled, and he didn't even remember what had caused the estrangement.

The emotional impact of getting involved

Even if we experienced little conflict with our parents over the years, getting involved in their care will affect us emotionally, especially as they become more dependent. We can never be fully prepared to parent our parents. Our emotions may lead us to resist entering their lives in this way, instead relying on professionals like their lawyer, doctor, or financial manager to handle the necessary details. What we cannot escape, though, is that our parents really do need us to play a primary role in their care. Many of us believe that we have a moral and personal responsibility to ensure that their needs are met.

Whether our involvement with them happens quickly or over many years, it is never easy to see our parents decline. We are sad when we see them walking more slowly or with canes and walkers. Their once strong voices weaken, and they strain to hear what we are saying. We're embarrassed when we see food stains on their clothes or when we smell odors coming from a dirty bathroom.

On the other hand, if they are in a nursing care facility, we likely have mixed feelings when we visit. We are relieved that they are getting the physical care they need from the staff and that the facility is bright and clean. However, we dread entering halls filled with people who may be worse off than our parents.

Perhaps the most painful experience for us is when our parent develops some form of dementia. For some, the decline is slow, and for others, it happens more quickly. What makes it harder to accept is that many are still physically healthy. At first, we try to ignore their forgetfulness or blank expressions, thinking they just had a bad day. But when the episodes increase and normal conversations become impossible, we are confronted with the reality that our parent is alive physically but not mentally. It is especially hard when they no longer recognize us. If our other parent is the caregiver, we worry about how this change affects them.

This kind of scenario happened to Greg. His father, Jim, had always been a high energy, outgoing businessman—optimistic even until his death. He was physically strong and athletic. When Greg's mother first mentioned that she was noticing some forgetfulness and disorientation in Jim, he and his siblings minimized her concerns. No one wanted to accept this change in their father. When Jim's health declined further, the family supported admitting Jim to a nursing care facility. It was difficult for Greg to watch as Alzheimer's disease progressed in Jim.

One of their most painful moments came when the family celebrated Jim's seventy-ninth and final birthday. The grandchildren had made birthday cards, only to witness him tear them up as he opened them. It was especially difficult for Greg to comfort his six-year-old daughter and explain why Grandpa tore up, in her words, "the most beautiful card I had ever made." It was impossible to prepare for this moment.

Caregiving tools

- **Care plan:** A written understanding that spells out the caregiver's specific responsibilities. It is based partly on the senior's wishes and needs and partly on the realities of their situation. The plan covers finances, housing, health, daily activities, and end-of-life needs. It indicates who is to do specific tasks and who is to coordinate the plan. It serves as a point of reference when difficult choices confront the family later on. (See Exhibit A on page 172)

- **Observing:** Caregivers are another set of eyes and ears for parents. We may be more objective than they can be about the early changes that we see. Typically, they aren't aware of their gradual changes, and spouses may even cover up for each other. Sometimes their friends are the first to alert us to what they observe, including their driving, housekeeping, or even to bruises that they can't explain.

- **Approaching:** Caregivers need to be sensitive when expressing concerns to parents. Asking them questions may be more effective than making statements that sound judgmental. Searching *together* for answers can be the most helpful.

- **Coordinating:** Caregivers will establish a relationship with their parent's medical doctor, lawyer, financial advisor, and all others who are involved in their care to assure that the parent's situation is properly managed. Though the need for care is minimal during the earliest stages of decline, it is helpful to begin this process before the needs become greater. Typically, one of us serves as the coordinator.

- **Advocating:** Caregivers ensure that the services our parents need are available and provided, especially if they are still living independently. This may require completing paperwork and accompanying them to appointments. Sharing your observations with the team members and asking questions can be helpful.

- **Assisting:** Caregivers may assist with transporting, monitoring medications, grocery shopping, and housework. Most of all, we will provide emotional support through visits, phone calls, and emails. Expressions of comfort through words and physical touch are the most basic kinds of care. As their conditions decline, direct involvement will increase, tending more to their daily needs and ensuring that supportive services are in place. Even those of us who live in another community will want to increase our involvement through phone calls and frequent visits.

- **Self-caring:** In the midst of giving care to others, it is important that we care for ourselves. The average time that an elderly person requires care is five years, and most caregivers wait approximately four years to ask for help from siblings or agencies. For our own health, we must share the responsibilities with others. Most of all, we need to set aside time for ourselves.

Ending thoughts

When our parents enter their senior years, most of them are in good health. We don't worry much about them. We are preoccupied with our own lives, and our parents seem comfortable in theirs. We know that, at some point, we should talk with them about the changes that are coming, but we usually wait for them to bring it up. Perhaps none of us wants to have this discussion. We know we should start talking, but we tell ourselves that we will when we have to.

But we can't keep denying that inner voice that says we should get started now—before our parents are in a crisis. If we have siblings, we need to begin talking *now* to plan ahead for the caregiving that is to come. We know that, when we join hands with our parents early, we will experience a sense of comfort when the end draws near. Having been a part of the journey throughout their senior years will make our lives more complete.

Indeed, caring for other persons, whether our parents, relatives, or friends, is the essence of what it means to be human. Giving and receiving are at the core of what living is all about. Good Samaritan stories have enriched the human community from its beginning. Benevolence is our highest and noblest attribute. When the persons we cared for die, we can be grateful to have been a part of a sacred experience.

Thinking and Planning Ahead

1. Find opportunities to share changes you have observed with your parents/aging adults and other care team members.

2. Be sensitive to their losses, and encourage your aging adult to talk about them.

3. Accept the importance of your role as a care team member.

4. If there are differences involving your parents, what steps can be taken to resolve them?

5. What can you do to keep yourself healthy while serving as a caregiver?

6. If you are a caregiver who is not an adult child, how much authority do you have? Be open and willing to discuss this with the aging adult and other care team members.

7. How do you handle opposition that might come from extended family members?

Conversations About Finances

MOM: *Some of our friends are buying a place in Florida where they can spend the winter. Now that we're retired, why don't we join them? Maybe they have more money than we do, but can't we do something a little special? We could at least rent a place for a few weeks? Retirement has to have some rewards.*

DAD: *The stock market keeps going up and down and I wonder what that will mean for our investments. I'm just a little uneasy about spending lots of money right now. I know we're not old yet, but you never know what could happen. I wish you would take more interest in our finances so you can see what I'm talking about. I know those papers from the mutual funds are hard to understand, but I worry what you would do if you had to take over the finances.*

DAUGHTER: *Did you talk with Mom and Dad lately? Mom talks like she wants to buy a place in Florida and says that*

Dad worries too much about money. Now that they are retired, she thinks there should be some rewards for all their hard work. But what really worries me is that Mom doesn't know anything about their finances. Dad does all the banking and pays the bills, and I don't know what she'd do if he died.

SON: *To be honest, I don't have any idea about their finances either. They both had good jobs and were putting money away somewhere. You'd think that they could take some trips or do something special. But when I brought up their finances to Dad, he brushed me off. He said they're okay. I got the impression that he didn't want me nosing into their business.*

NEPHEW: *Last week Uncle Charlie went out and bought a new RV and is planning to take a trip to Alaska. I understand why he wants to do that, but I wonder if he can afford to spend that much money. The worst thing is that he asked me to be his financial power of attorney, and he still hasn't shown me his financial records. I guess I'll have to talk with him.*

By the time we retire, many of us have a degree of financial security that we had not known before. Typically, our debt is gone. We have our investments in place and retirement plans that provide some income. We may work part time to supplement monthly retirement or Social Security checks. If nothing unexpected comes up, we can look forward to some good times. Finally—or so it seems—we can relax and take comfort in what we have accomplished.

Yet most of us are faced with living on a fixed income. Gone are the days of pay raises, bonuses, and profit sharing. We can no longer count on extra money from job promotions. We know that we are required to begin withdrawing some of our investments soon after we turn seventy, and that will give us some extra money. But we don't like the idea that we might have to use that money for day-to-day expenses. From our first job to our last, we always expected to earn more money. Those days are gone forever.

Now we must think twice about large purchases and optional spending. Some of our friends still had outstanding debt when they retired, including mortgages and credit card balances. Nearly 20 percent of us declare bankruptcy.[1] We tend to have less money in savings than past generations had. It is hard not to worry where the money will come from for house repairs or for long-term medical care.

We have to take a second look at the appeals for money from our alma mater and charities that we supported in the past. With less money to give to worthy causes, we feel some sadness, even guilt, when we toss their appeals away. We realize that we have less influence on important causes now that we can't contribute the way we used to. Sometimes our names are left off the banquet fundraiser lists that we were invited to before.

We are becoming aware that we are facing our financial future alone and left to deal with the consequences of how we prepared for this moment. In past generations, seniors turned to adult children or other family members if they ran out of resources. But most of us won't be able to do that anymore. We can only hope that Social Security and our investments will be enough to meet our needs—maybe for twenty or more years.

Shared responsibility

In some groups, parents and adult children remain financially interconnected. Bishop Lawrence says that in his particular African American community, finances are openly shared within the extended family. There is a belief that what's mine is yours, especially in low- and middle-income families. In these families, there are few secrets and a great deal of interdependence. On the other hand, persons who have a greater amount of wealth have become more private and individualistic about their money. They may be especially wary of others in their community who might want to be "taken care of" by them.

Lawrence's wife, Nereida, told us about her experiences in her Latin American community, where families display a great deal of openness about finances, especially when several generations live together. They have no financial secrets. Few bother to have wills, perhaps because they have limited assets. After their parents die, most families simply distribute any assets among themselves. Sometimes the process doesn't work well. Her father tried to talk with his adult children about finances but was never able to follow through with his plans. She and Lawrence believe it may take another generation to develop new patterns of handling their assets.

Beginning the financial conversation

In many North American families today, finances are not discussed by parents until they are in a crisis. For some, those discussions happen after we die, when the will is probated. We can do better. Wouldn't it be more helpful if our adult children or substitutes became co-managers of our finances early in our retirement years? That would mean fully disclosing our finances to them and welcoming their opinions. It may not be easy at first, but if we invite them to partner with us now, we will all be more comfortable later on when we really need them. This partnership can bring peace of mind to all of us and reduce the chance that we will make mistakes or that there will be conflict in our family over finances.

Their involvement may help protect us from scams, unwise investments, and questionable sales pitches. While those of us over sixty-five are only one-eighth of the US population, one-third of scam victims are seniors.[2] As we age, our brains do not process information as fast or as objectively, making us more vulnerable to poor decision-making. We are especially susceptible to bad judgments when we're mentally fatigued late in the day, a time when scammers typically call. Knowing that we should run any requests by our co-managers can prevent us from making bad decisions. Slowing the process down is an important protection.

Difficulties with getting started

Among the important things seniors and their planning partners need to talk about, money is one of the most difficult. For most of us, money is a very private matter. When we were raising our children, not many of us talked with them about money. Whether we thought they wouldn't understand, that being open with them would make them worry if things were tight, or make them feel superior if we had more, we just kept them in the dark. Whatever the case, money talks were rare for most families. Some studies confirm that few of us invite our adult children to talk about our finances.[3] But in our senior years, we need to have these discussions because we now *need* their help.

That is particularly hard to understand, considering how frustrated some of us were by our own parents' lack of openness. When they had a medical crisis, developed dementia, or died, we were left with very little or no guidance to find important papers, open lock boxes, or contact financial agents. Sometimes we even had to settle their debts. Those of us who went through this experience vowed we would never let that happen to the persons who have to settle *our* estates.

Unfortunately many of us have not changed direction. An American doctor trapped in a fallen building during the 2010 earthquake in Haiti shouted out to a reporter, "I've got to get out of here to get my estate in order. My kids will never forgive me if they have to take care of my papers." She probably spoke for many of us.

Reasons some parents hold back

Why do we resist talking about our finances? First, talking openly about *anything* is hard to do because we are entering a period of decline. We are losing health, power, purpose, place, and dignity. Turning to our adult children to discuss finances can feel like one more loss. Second, if we as spouses disagree about finances, we don't want our helpers to know that, especially if knowing about it would put them in the middle. Third, if we have managed poorly or have limited resources, we may not want our adult children to know because we are embarrassed. Fourth, if we have accumulated significant wealth, we don't want them to know because then they may pressure us to give at least some of it to them now. Fifth, we want to postpone any potential family feuds over money until we are gone.

The importance of becoming a team

Being convinced that there is a better way, we must initiate conversations about finances with our adult children or a substitute early in our senior years. Most of these conversations will be informal and unscheduled. That might include brief phone/email exchanges about sudden unexpected expenses or even a surprise gift from a relative's estate. We may also want to chat about some of the purchases we are thinking of making.

At some point, we will schedule a more formal meeting with the family. At this meeting, we will select our executor and financial power of attorney. A written statement of our assets, liabilities, and income will be presented to everyone. Minutes will be kept and distributed, including to family members who cannot or who choose not to attend. Opinions of all members will be heard and consensus sought. Meeting as a family ensures that no one person can have an unfair or unwise influence on us. If conflict emerges that can't be resolved, it may be helpful to invite a counselor to mediate. Any financial changes should be discussed with our attorney and financial advisor. Family meetings should be scheduled periodically or as needed.

Harry was fortunate to get the family farm at a good price. However, when he sold it to developers many years later, he felt it was only right to share the significant profit with his siblings. He calculated the fair-market price at the time he purchased the farm, including interest that would have accrued. Needless to say, his siblings were grateful and surprised with his generosity. He can attend family gatherings with no regrets. The family is at peace.

Challenges from divorce and remarriage

If we are divorced, our adult children often experience challenges regarding our finances. Divorce typically shatters family ties and tends to impact our assets negatively.

Decisions about assets are made under pressure and in an adversarial legal environment that can pit divorcing spouses against each other. That atmosphere can over-shadow our better financial judgment. Adult children tend to be caught in the middle between conflicting parents, making their role as co-managers difficult if not impossible.

The situation becomes even more complex when parents remarry, often blending two families together. If we are young when we remarry, we may create a third family, which can create additional complications. It becomes especially challenging if one spouse brings more wealth into the marriage than the other or if prenuptial agreements were not worked out in advance.

Facing increased medical expenses

Because most of us are living longer, we'll likely face significant medical expenses throughout our senior years. That can include the deductibles for medications, medical tests and procedures, and doctor visits. It can even include some equipment that we need, such as wheelchairs.

For some of us, the expenses are significant when we need long-term residential nursing care or multiple shifts for in-home care. An estimated 40 percent of us will be admitted to a nursing care facility before we die.[4] That includes those who need short-term rehabilitation for joint replacements and other temporary care.

The average stay in nursing care facilities is two years, commonly costing $100,000 or more per year.[5] Medicare pays only a small portion of that cost. If all of our assets are depleted, most facilities accept Medicaid as payment. For those of us who gave our adult children monetary assets during the five years before we applied for Medicaid, the government can require that they repay some or all of those costs depending on the specific circumstances. It is important that we check with a lawyer about this potential liability.

Some of us choose to enter a continuing care retirement community because they have nursing care facilities for us when our health declines. The average entrance fee to these multilevel communities is around $200,000 per couple.[6] The fee varies depending on the size of the unit chosen and other amenities. There is also a sizable monthly charge while we are living on the campus. The entrance fees help subsidize the unpaid costs that Medicaid or other sources don't fully cover for residents in the nursing care unit.

Various long-term healthcare insurance plans meet some of the costs of nursing care. The plans can be complex, so it is important to know what they cover. Most have limitations and the premiums can be costly, especially when we have reduced income after retirement. In the words of one financial adviser, "People who really need the insurance can't afford it, and those who can afford it don't really need it." Some insurance companies are no longer writing long-term care policies because the cost of care is rising too fast.

It is important to ask our adult children to help us make a decision about this kind of insurance. When Don and Anna first considered long-term insurance, they discovered that it would be expensive because of their advanced age. This prompted them to discuss the matter with their daughter, Jane, who assured them that when they needed care, they'd have a place in her home. Having seen her parents care for her maternal grandmother in their home for eight years served as a good model.

Because of the offer from Jane, Don and Anna chose a plan that pays some of the costs of in-home medical care.

The savings that came from that decision made it possible for Don and Anna to set up an investment plan that will benefit church agencies and other charities in the future. That is especially remarkable considering that they spent most of their adult lives working for various church programs, including twenty years as missionaries in Africa.

Loss of wealth in the broader society

In previous generations some wealth was transferred to heirs in the form of farms or family businesses. Today, fewer of us are connected with those assets. Typically we work in various professions or are wage earners and unable to accumulate large amounts of wealth to pass on to heirs. At the same time, most of us live in comfortable homes, have multiple cars, travel extensively, and have expensive hobbies. Even though we each had a career and have some form of pension or retirement accounts, some of these assets can't be passed on to our adult children. In addition, our longer life span means medical expenses and institutional care can deplete whatever reserves we still may have. The implications of these changes are enormous for our adult children and the various charities that depend on our generosity.

Death expenses

Although in the larger picture funeral costs may not be a major financial item, they can still be significant. It is not unusual for funerals to cost more than $10,000,[7] so when both parents die, $20,000 is an impressive amount that is taken from the estate. Many funeral directors are helpful in finding ways to reduce costs, and most have plans that allow for prepayment as a way of avoiding these sudden costs at the time of the death.

Emotions at the time of the death can influence us toward choosing expensive funerals as a way of honoring our loved ones We may feel embarrassed if we choose a less expensive casket. Sometimes, family members have differences over how much should be spent for the funeral, the cemetery, and even about the costs of the memorial stone. Increasing numbers of seniors are choosing cremation, in part to reduce the costs of the funeral and the burial. However, not all family members are comfortable with this choice. It is important that we begin conversations about all of these things with our adult children while we are in good health and before emotions influence our decisions.

Death of the first parent

Sometimes we neglect to plan for the financial changes that will arise after the death of a spouse. Can we survive financially when we lose their pension or Social Security check? Is that counterbalanced by the elimination of the costs that might have been spent for their care? Did they have a life insurance policy? If the spouse who died was the financial manager, will we be able to learn this new task?

The older we are when we lose our spouse, the more help we will need from our co-managers. When we become a widow(er), it is then that many of us reach out to our adult children for the first time. Often it is about finances. Much of our discomfort could have been prevented if we had involved our adult children or someone in their place much earlier. The death of a spouse is already very traumatic. Worrying about finances should not be an additional burden that we have to carry alone.

Remarriage

After a death or divorce, some of us will remarry. Our new spouse may have more or fewer assets than we do or have spending patterns that are different than ours. In addition, problems can arise if we handle finances with our adult children in contrasting ways. All of this can create conflict in the new marriage and between the separate sets of adult children. That is why we must determine before we remarry which assets we will share with our new spouse and which we will keep separate. Understanding these differences is important.

As we enter a courtship with a new partner, we should consult our adult children to ensure that we are making wise decisions about this relationship. Obviously, the older we are when we start dating, the more our children should be involved. Sometimes we remarry because we are lonely and emotionally fragile and aren't objective about the decisions we are making. That is why we need help to develop a wise financial plan. It is essential to create a prenuptial agreement with the help of our lawyer. In most situations, we should have our adult children remain involved in co-managing our separate and individual funds throughout the new marriage.

Karen and Mike remarried when they were in their sixties. Both had spouses who died some years earlier. Because Karen brought greater financial assets into the new marriage, she and Mike consulted a financial advisor and a lawyer to distribute the assets of their deceased spouses fairly. The plan designated that one-third of Karen's assets would be placed into an income-producing trust for her adult children, one-third would be given to designated charities, and the remainder would be brought into the common household purse for her and Mike's use. They also decided that Mike's assets would go to his children.

Creating a financial file

To help our adult children understand and co-manage our
finances, we should list the following:

- All assets, including properties and possessions.
  Items of particular value, such as heirlooms and
  valuable artwork, should be appraised.
- Life insurance policies with policy numbers, premiums, and dates of maturity, beneficiaries, agents,
  and other important information. Remember to
  include phone numbers and addresses.
- Other assets such as stocks, bonds, mutual funds,
  annuities, and bank accounts should be noted with
  appropriate identifiers.
- Additional sources of income, including Social Security and pensions. Records of recent yearly earnings
  for five to seven years can be helpful.
- All liabilities, including debts, mortgages, mem-
  bership agreements, maintenance fees, property
  taxes, credit card balances, and home equity loans.
  Account numbers, payment dates, and balances are
  important to record.
- Access codes and passwords are essential for all
  accounts.

In most families each child should have a copy of this information and know where to find the original documents.
Having it in one location gives everyone peace of mind and
ensures a better outcome. Some financial advisors recom-
mend having it stored in a three-ring binder. (See exhibits
B, C, and D on pages 174–181.)

At the age of seventy-two, Sam suffered a fatal heart
attack while driving with his wife to a family cabin in the
mountains in northern Pennsylvania. Ruth was severely
injured in the accident and spent three months in the

hospital and rehab centers. Naturally, their three daughters were traumatized, grief-stricken, and left with the heavy responsibility of settling their father's estate, while providing emotional and practical support to their mother.

One of the tasks that fell to them was making financial decisions for their mother. Their father had kept good financial records. But it would have been easier for them if they had been given an orientation to his system. They had some difficulty, for example, tracking down life insurance information, beneficiaries, and other data that was filed in different places. Later they learned how his system works and can now assist their mother in decision-making. Things can come to a standstill if our adult children don't have the facts they need or know where to find pertinent information.

It is wise to consult with an attorney about the best place to keep important papers. Regulations vary from state to state regarding who may have access to a safe deposit box and under what circumstances. It probably is not essential to store photocopies of a will or other estate planning documents in a safe deposit box or a fireproof box. Storing originals there may be a good safeguard, but not all counterparts of original power of attorney documents or living wills should be stored in a locked location because the family may need prompt access to the documents. Some lawyers suggest that a copy of our wills and advance directives be stored at home for immediate access. Marriage and drivers' licenses, birth certificates, and copies of social security numbers can be stored in a firebox or safe deposit box.

The adult(s) whom a parent names as agent(s) in a power of attorney document should be informed on where to obtain keys and passwords. When the one who granted the power wishes to pass control to the agent(s), s/he should give the agent(s) the keys and passwords. It is important to consider that some children do not have the skills or perspective to justify giving them access to these documents. If several children have such access, they may take inconsistent actions. Choose your agents wisely.

Wills

Many of us have had a will for a long time. However, there are some people who delay or avoid having a will because they have limited assets. Perhaps they don't know how important it is to have one. Maryanne was confronted with this situation when serving as financial power of attorney for a single aunt. Originally, her mother served in this role and was also named as the beneficiary of a $5,000 life insurance policy intended to cover funeral costs for the aunt. However, when Maryanne's mother died, the aunt asked Maryanne to serve as financial power of attorney and was listed as the beneficiary of the life insurance policy. It wasn't until her aunt died that Maryanne discovered there was no will and thus no executor. That meant Maryanne had no authority to proceed with financial matters, including claiming the life insurance benefits. To settle the matter, Maryanne had to engage an attorney. The importance of having a will cannot be overstated. Failing to do so creates undue stress and extra expense.

Retirement is a time to update our will. It is now suggested that we review and update wills every five years because circumstances may change, and state and federal laws also change. This ensures that assets will be distributed to heirs as we intend, and that the will strives for an outcome that all parties will perceive as fair or reasonable. We should also be sure that charities are represented as we wish.

When we have an adult child who is physically or intellectually challenged, it is important to plan ahead for his or her future. Various survivorship care arrangements can be made with the help of an attorney. Such plans usually name an administrator of the assets who oversees the child's care. Involving the other siblings in the decision-making is essential.

Some attorneys suggest itemizing in a memorandum a detailed list of personal and household effects that shall pass to designated individuals. This memo can be referenced in a will that validates that the latest signed and dated version of the memo is in control.

A will should name an executor to carry out instructions in the will. In some states, the law gives relatives or beneficiaries the opportunity to be appointed to administer the estate. If none of them will serve, a court will choose and appoint a bank to administer the estate when the will is probated.

The authority held by an agent with power of attorney is defined in the power of attorney document. This person(s) may be granted legal authority to sign documents, write checks, and make legal and financial decisions on our behalf when we are no longer able to.

Many factors go into the determination of whether to appoint several persons (and whether each has individual authority or whether they must act jointly) or whether the document should appoint one or more alternates. With express mail and email, it generally is not difficult to arrange for signatures of someone who is at a distance, although proximity is convenient.

A person who is nominated as executor in a will has no authority to act until the person is appointed by the probate court, which will issue a certificate evidencing authority to act for the estate of the deceased.

The same or a different person(s) can be designated as a medical agent who holds power of attorney or medical proxy for each of us. That person is directed to implement the instructions in a living will. A living will typically provides that, consistent with such instructions, the agent shall decide matters for which the living will does not set forth directions.

We encourage parents to be open with their children about their finances and their wishes regarding life-extending medical procedures. That may result in less conflict when a crisis develops, although not necessarily so.

The National Physician's Order for Life Sustaining Treatment (POLST) Paradigm is designed to determine the kind of care that people receive at the end of life. You may want to ask that your living will includes authority for a health care agent to request a POLST, and then that a designated agent or proxy carries out the instructions.

Estate

Those of us who have acquired significant wealth through real estate, businesses, farms, or investments enjoy the comforts that they can bring. Financial security enables our children to be broadened by travel, education, and living in comfortable homes in good neighborhoods. At the same time, we receive the rewards that come from sharing our resources with charities and individuals in need. The proverb that it is better to give than to receive can be a part of the family legacy.

Whatever the size of our estate, it is important that we seek counsel from a lawyer and financial advisor about how to manage these resources. We may wish to consult an elder-law attorney, who focuses especially on resource planning at this time in our lives. Independent advice is important for our financial security while we are living and can be invaluable when settling our estates.

Each family releases their assets in their own ways. Most pass a portion of them on to their children in equal shares. Many designate a charity to receive a share similar to that of the adult children. Some children encourage their parents to give a larger portion of their estate to charity because they are doing well financially and don't need a great deal of help.

Planning well for the distribution of assets can result in endless good feelings. Dottie remembers her parents as generous people who shared their financial resources with others, including their own children and grandchildren. She especially appreciated that her parents checked with her first before giving the grandchildren a gift of money. Her father involved her and her brother in planning for succession of leadership in the family business. He had lost his mother when he was seventeen, so perhaps that made him more careful to have a plan in place before he died.

The family established a foundation so that, if the business was sold, some of the proceeds could be distributed to various charitable organizations, church agencies, and community projects. Her parents, the adult children, and in-laws were all named directors to manage the foundation and distribute grants annually. The family members meet quarterly to review the investments and make decisions about the distribution of funds.

With some of their inheritance, the one couple created a benevolent account within the larger foundation. It has been in place for more than thirty years and continues a family legacy of stewardship. They say, "It has become part of who we are to share resources with others." It is gratifying to observe how that passion of giving to others is being passed on to their children and grandchildren. Their humility and generosity are models for everyone.

Ending thoughts

Some of us have enough wealth to share with others throughout our lives or after we die. Others may have smaller assets to pass on to children, grandchildren, or other heirs. However, because many of us live longer and need medical and institutional care, our assets are used up by the time we die.

It is important that, early in our senior years, we team up with our adult children or substitutes and develop a financial plan that anticipates our needs and wishes for this last stage of our lives. We need these teammates for their broader view of our financial situation and to help us make the best decisions, especially when we begin to lose our mental capacity.

We welcome our adult children or substitute into a partnership with us. We will provide full disclosure of our assets and liabilities to each member. Together, we name one of them to be our financial power of attorney to handle our finances when we can no longer do so and one to be the executor who will help settle our estate when we die. The family will partner with our financial advisor and our attorney to ensure that the best decisions are being made.

When conflict exists within the family, a professional counselor will be engaged to resolve the differences. The goal is to ensure that the family reaches this important time at peace with each other. We want to leave this life with our finances in order. More importantly, we want to leave with our relationships in order.

Thinking and Planning Ahead

1. Retirement is a good time for parents to involve their adult children in financial planning.
2. If seniors have no adult children, it is important to find a reliable person to partner with them.
3. Resolving conflict within the family brings many rewards.
4. What are our options if we feel our children aren't trustworthy?
5. How open should we be if one child receives more than the others?
6. What are the benefits of having a prenuptial agreement?

Where to Live

SON: *I think we've got to talk with Mom and Dad about selling their house. Today when I drove by, I saw Dad up on the roof doing something with the chimney. I know he's only seventy, but he's not as steady as he used to be. And the yard is beginning to look a little bit out of control with crab grass and dandelions. But every time I mention something to him about moving to a place where maintenance is provided, he gets defensive.*

DAUGHTER: *Mom's the same way. She gets real sentimental when I talk with her about leaving the house. She has all these memories of when we were growing up there. Seeing us off to school, our birthdays, and she can't stand the thought of us not being able to be together there for Thanksgiving. I do worry what would happen to them if they had to move. I know they don't want to go to a retirement community.*

DAD: *I'm really feeling pressure from the kids. This idea that I can't be up on the roof to fix the chimney is silly. I* *feel as strong as ever, and I know how to handle heights. What do they want us to do? If we get someone in to do all of the repairs on this place, we'll run out of money. These retirement communities that they keep talking about would drive me crazy. I'd have nothing to do. Shuffleboard doesn't interest me, and eating in the dining room with all those people isn't for me!*

MOM: *I don't think they understand what this place means to us. When I tell them about all the memories, they shrug and say, "You can't live in the past." They promise to visit if we move to a retirement center and have holiday dinners at their place. I am not ready for that kind of move—it's just too early.*

NIECE: *I keep worrying about Aunt Barbara living in that big house all alone since Uncle Charlie died. She says she's only eighty and can take care of the place, especially since she found a neighbor boy to mow the grass. Her children call every week and seem concerned. It might be easier if she moved in with us, but shouldn't her family take care of her?*

Deciding where to live during our senior years can be difficult. If we live long enough, many of us will reside at several places before we die. Most of us are deeply attached to our homes, and it is hard to think about moving. It is the place where we raised our children, returned to after hard days at work, celebrated birthdays, and mourned the loss of loved ones. This home is a repository of important memories. We are reluctant to give it up. Walter Brueggemann says, "Place is space that has historical meanings, and where some things have happened that are now remembered and that provide continuity and identity across generations."[1]

Perhaps the most painful thing about leaving our home is that it symbolizes an ending to an important stage in our life. For many of us, the future seems empty and perhaps without purpose.

Now more than in past generations, we find the decision about where to live to be much more complicated, in part because we are living longer and have many more options available to us. In the past, our ancestors died much younger, and the surviving spouse usually was taken in by an adult child. Even when both parents lived to an old age, they were cared for by the family. People who had no children usually lived alone until they died or went to "old folk's homes." Now some still remain in their home or move to a smaller place. Some go to a continuing care community.

Even if we have adult children, we face some challenges if they live in other communities. If we move close to where they are, it is likely that none of our friends will be in that community, and it would mean starting over with doctors, shopping, and social activities. Besides, being close to our children could place a heavy burden on them at a busy time in their lives—something we don't want to do.

Dealing with our possessions

Many of us delay making a decision about moving simply because we don't know what to do with our possessions. What if the place we are moving to has less space? For some of us, the greatest challenge is emotional. We feel deeply attached to what we have, like the favorite chair that we can't take with us. Some of our resistance is sentimental. Maybe we don't really need ten suits or jewelry that we haven't worn for years. Or maybe it is a library full of books

that we no longer read. These things have memories connected to them, and we find it hard to see them go. It's like
we are giving pieces of ourselves away.

Fortunately, we can take some of our things with us.
The things we can't sell, we can give to our family or to
a charity. It makes the losses hurt less if adult children,
grandchildren, or other family members want them. We
get a sense of satisfaction when we see an heirloom quilt
on their bed, a grandchild playing with our old train set, or
an ancestor's clock on their mantel. Giving up driving may
be easier when we transfer our car to a granddaughter who
needs it for her job.

However, it can be painful when no one wants the things
we cherish. Family members may not want them because
their decorating tastes are different. Our fancy dinnerware
can't be put in a dishwasher. The old china cupboard would
look out of place in their home. Sometimes they don't want
our things simply because they lack the space for them. As
hard as it may be, some items will need to be thrown away.
Some of us can't fathom reducing our possessions because
we are hoarders. Items fill up our garages, attics, base-
ments, and storage sheds.

We should start sorting through our possessions before
we even think about moving. The older we are when we
start the process, the more challenging it can be. Sorting
through pictures and other treasures often brings back
pleasant memories. Consulting with our adult children
and distributing possessions early makes us better prepared for our upcoming move. We then have the pleasure
of knowing that they are enjoying them. To make the distribution fair, we can send pictures of the items to all family members and have them pick a number to determine
who goes first.

New developments that influence housing choices

It has become increasingly possible for us to remain in our homes longer. Aging-in-place services now provide in-home nursing and personal care that can postpone the need to move. In addition, with the expansion of in-home hospice care, it can even be possible to remain in our home through the dying process. These services can prevent unnecessary hospitalizations and may also delay admission to nursing care facilities. In fact, one of the mandates of governmental agencies on aging is to provide in-home services that make it possible for some persons who are in nursing-care facilities to return to their homes.

Concurrent with these community-based services is the growth of high-tech equipment designed to monitor our health and safety at home. Call bracelets can contact emergency personnel when we are unable to make a phone call. Other technology reveals whether we are taking medications correctly, reducing the high number of seniors hospitalized from medication errors. Additional devices check our blood pressure and blood sugar levels. And more are being developed every day.

Discussing housing with our adult children or substitute

Making the right choice about housing is complicated, and the options can be confusing. Our emotions and those of our adult children can get in the way of making these decisions. Various studies show that 80 percent of us say that we want to stay in our homes as long as possible, but few of us have given much thought to other possibilities. It doesn't seem to be on our adult children's minds either. However, these conversations need to take place and in a spirit of mutual respect. All of us will be impacted by the decisions that are made or *not* made. Developing a plan for the future is necessary. The following factors are important to consider:

- our age
- our health status
- whether both of us are living
- size, condition, and adaptability of our current property
- cost of maintaining the property
- proximity and availability of family
- access to community services
- transportation needs
- our financial status
- personal preferences
- knowledge of all options

As a part of the conversation, it is important to assess safety and mobility features in our present house and in any future setting. These features include wheelchair accessibility, outside entrances with no steps, and first-floor living that provides both a bedroom and bathroom. Having these accommodations may reduce the need for seniors to move to other settings prematurely. Dr. Kimberly Stoeckel found in her research that 47 percent of persons over fifty-five were unable to identify any possible barriers to safety and mobility in their present setting when in fact the barriers were there. Of that group, 75 percent indicated no plans to move to another place.[2]

Clearly, the healthier and wealthier we are, the more choices we have for where to live. Regardless of our status at the beginning of our senior years, changes can take place later that make it necessary to move. Typically, we'll make several housing changes before we die. Part of the discussion should include an ongoing assessment of our ability to handle the tasks of daily living, including cooking, cleaning, self-care, and possibly giving care to our spouse. Can we find someone to mow our lawn or provide laundry and cleaning services when needed? Can family members help us with any of these tasks?

One of the realities influencing housing choices is our financial situation. At the time we begin our discussions, it is hard to predict the future worth of our home and investments. What we can do, though, is learn the prices for all of the alternative housing situations. We should also check on the costs of in-home care. Talking about the reality of our finances and possible expenses helps shape our housing decision.

Option 1: Stay where we are as long as possible

For many of us, there is no compelling reason to leave our homes, especially if we are in reasonably good health and are able to do the necessary tasks or to have them provided for us.

Earl and Vera, when in their mid-eighties, continued to find enjoyment working in their garden and flowerbeds. Earl got satisfaction from mowing their yard on a riding mower. Vera kept their property immaculate and their flower gardens filled with variety and color. Weeds could not be found anywhere. From their living room window, they enjoyed the view of the pond on the farm where they used to live. They valued hosting many family events in their recreation room. It was only when their health began to decline that they chose to move into an assisted care unit. Their family supported that decision.

Many of us don't want to leave our home place because it is filled with pleasant memories. It is still a good gathering place for the extended family and for entertaining friends. The familiar grocery store is just around the corner. The doctor's office is a five-minute drive away. Some of us aren't ready to give up our walks through the town park, the church where we have been longtime members, or to move away from our neighborhood friends. Our brains depend on familiarity.

To make it possible to stay, we can change the house to accommodate our needs. We install grab bars in the bathrooms, put in showers that accommodate wheelchairs, and remove loose rugs that could cause a fall. We consider installing motorized stair chairs to allow us to move from floor to floor. Perhaps most important of all, we access aging-in-place services in our communities. We also receive some support from family and friends.

Some of us have informal arrangements with our neighbors. When Menno's wife died, he made an agreement with his neighbor that she would call him if his kitchen window shade remained drawn in the morning. That plan worked well for a number of years. Later, when his health declined significantly, Menno's family began to provide more day-to-day care.

The availability of family members to provide some care has a direct impact on our ability to remain at home. Adult children who live nearby can check on us from time to time and assist in a variety of ways. But we must recognize that, as our health declines, another plan will be needed. Many of our adult children have careers and families who need them. Those who live in other communities can provide support by phone or on their occasional visits, but it may not be enough.

Option 2: Move to a smaller place

For many of us, the place where we live is too big and expensive to maintain. Housekeeping is beyond what we can comfortably manage. The yard and other maintenance requirements are too strenuous—maybe even dangerous. Some of us leave our home simply because we have lost interest in doing so much work. Moving to a smaller house, condo, or apartment that requires less care becomes appealing.

Moving to a smaller place can allow us to remain in an age-diverse community, maintain independence, and reduce our housing costs. We have access to home-based medical and community services. Remaining in the community enables us to continue meaningful connections with family and friends.

When John and Janet were sixty years old, they chose to leave the farmette where they had raised their family. They wanted to be free from the ongoing upkeep that the old farmhouse and property required. Although they are comfortable with their decision to move, they do miss their beautiful view of the meadow and the privacy of country living.

They moved into a new duplex in a development several miles from their previous home. At first, their adult children weren't enthusiastic about the change, in part because they wanted *their* children to enjoy the farm as much as they did while growing up. However, now that John and Janet are in a new place, they have more time to visit their family. When they gather in the new home, everyone is grateful for the finished basement where the grandchildren can play. The move made it necessary to get rid of some of their possessions, but they found it rewarding to return childhood treasures to their adult children. John and Janet enjoy being in a neighborhood that has a good mixture of families and retirees.

Option 3: Move to a 55+ community

Age-restricted communities sprang up in the Sun Belt as retreats for retirees, especially for winter use. In more recent years, these communities have become year-round residences, and this concept has spread to many other states. While comfort, recreation, low maintenance, and camaraderie with peers are their main purpose, some seniors like the fact that they are protected from the noise and frenzy—and crime—in the neighborhoods they left behind. Some residents feel even safer when the entrances are gated.

In most situations, the seniors retain ownership of the house but pay a monthly fee for services, including yard care and snow removal (for colder regions). Some associations offer clubhouses that organize activities and provide swimming pools. Some have private golf courses. The developments are meticulously managed and are aesthetically appealing.

Many of these communities have rules that limit the number of days that adult children and grandchildren can stay overnight. Although some residents like the fact that children aren't under their feet, others are bothered by the limitations placed on their families. They may also miss the friendships they had in their former community. Some of the 55+ communities may not have access to public transit and that can be a challenge when persons are no longer able to drive. A move to these communities may take seniors away from their family, limiting the support that they can provide.

Joanne experienced that situation with her parents, who left their lifelong home in the north to enter a 55+ community in Miami. At first, they enjoyed living in a carefree, warm, and sunny environment. When Joanne began noticing some cognitive and physical decline in her mother, she knew that the time had come for her parents to move closer to her. She was living in a community several hours away. When she brought up the subject, they resisted because they weren't ready to give up their independence. Now, Joanne is concerned about how she can assist them from that distance.

An additional option for older adults is the Village to Village Network, a movement that has sprung up in hundreds of places in the United States and in other countries. It is a virtual community in which members live in their own homes though scattered throughout towns and cities; some are even in rural areas. By paying an annual fee, members receive access to services through a village coordinator. Volunteers provide lawn mowing, transportation, grocery shopping, and other tasks. Villagers also receive a list of approved tradesmen who assist with home repairs and technical support. Perhaps most important are the social connections forged through shared activities and friendships.

Option 4: We move closer to adult children

Over the past several generations, more of our adult children have left our communities to study, pursue careers, or get a fresh start. This has left many of us to manage the senior years on our own. Perhaps as a response to that, some of us choose to move closer to where they are, in part to make caregiving easier for them. It also can deepen our relationship with them and with our grandchildren.

Marion and Verna spent most of their adult years in Oregon. After retirement, they made frequent visits to their daughter, Kristen, and her family in Pennsylvania. At her urging, they decided to make a permanent move to Lancaster. Their new home provides space for Kristen, her husband Johncey, and the three grandchildren when they come for meals and impromptu gatherings—even sleepovers. It also has become a special gathering place for all of the grandchildren to play together when Marion and Verna's son and his family come to visit from California.

The move to Pennsylvania has been rewarding for Marion and Verna despite the fact that they left long-term friends and the beauty of the Northwest behind. Now they treasure the opportunity to play a bigger part in the lives of their Pennsylvania grandchildren. At the same time, Kristen has supported her parents during their health challenges and hospitalizations. Marion and Verna have reunited with friends from college, made many new friends, and have found a supportive church community. They are both active in meaningful volunteer assignments and are involved in the rich cultural experiences in nearby cities.

Option 5: Adult child moves closer to us

Although it is less common, some adult children choose to move to the community where their parents live. This move may mean returning to where they grew up, where they have good memories, and where they can renew ties to old friends. While their primary motive is to be available to their parents, this time together can allow the development of deeper emotional connections within the family. A benefit for the adult children comes from having the parents provide free childcare, transport grandchildren to activities, or to check on their house when the family is on vacation.

After I (Gerald) had a medical crisis several years ago, our daughter Anne and her husband, Todd, were awakened to the fact that we were getting older. In addition, Todd's parents, who also live in this community, had some health challenges. Because of these changes, Anne and Todd felt it was time to move near all of us. They also chose to move to enable both sets of grandparents to be more involved with their grandchildren.

Todd has retained his dental practice in their former community, despite having a significant commute to his office. Anne has become a chaplain at a nearby continuing care facility. Our entire family, including Anne's siblings who live in this community, is convinced that the right move was made at the right time. It has been rewarding to have the entire family become part of our support network. Family gatherings have become rich times of bonding. Although we are in good health presently, the family knows that will change at some point.

Brian Castner, in the "My Turn" section of *Newsweek* in March 2007, wrote that, when he ended his career in the military, he and his wife had to decide where to put down roots and raise their three sons. At first, the most important criteria included living where there were trees and green grass, preferably somewhere in the eastern United States. They were tired of living in places around the world that had brown landscapes.

It eventually occurred to them that what they really wanted was for their children to grow up near their grandparents in Brian's hometown of Buffalo, New York, where they would also be near great-grandparents, aunts, uncles, and cousins. Brian realized he had taken his large supportive family for granted until this point. Some of his friends didn't understand why he wanted to move home. They said that Brian had seen too much of the world to move back to what they considered to be a small, predictable, boring town. Brian's reply was, "I have seen too much of the world *not* to move home."

Option 6: Three-generation living arrangements

Several generations ago, it was common for parents, adult children, and grandchildren to live in the same house, especially after one of the parents died. That pattern is still common among some ethnic groups in the United States—more commonly in Hispanic, African American, and Asian families. In many of these situations, the only privacy parents have is in their own bedroom. Living together may reflect economic necessity, but it is also a custom that continues from traditions practiced in their home countries, many of which hold the elderly in high esteem and consider them an integral part of the family.

Bishop Lawrence Chiles describes family life within many African American households: "We have our own version of the *grossdawdy* house. We just live in the same house—it doesn't matter how many people are there. There's always room for one more. The older generation helps to take care of the younger generation." When the parents' health declines, the roles are reversed, and the adult children become caregivers. Aging is seen as normal, and the life cycle from birth to death is a part of everyone's daily experience.

Sean Poulter, Consumer Affairs Editor for the *Daily Mail*, reported on February 16, 2016 that, in the United States, the number of three-generational households have increased by more than half in the past ten years including in white households. That translates to 16.6 percent of the population. Families are seeing this as a way to pool finances and a remedy for isolation in old age. The benefits of interactions between the generations are significant and express the valuing of interdependence more than independence.

Families move together at different points in their lives and for differing reasons. Harold and Mary realized it was time to turn over their farm to one of their sons and were exploring the possibility of entering a continuing care retirement community. At about the same time, another one of their sons, Steve, and his wife, Marilyn, were making plans to build a house on the property for themselves. When Marilyn heard about her in-laws' intentions, she suggested that an apartment be added onto the new house for Harold and Mary. They were surprised by the offer and pleased to remain among family members and in the neighborhood that was special to them.

Marilyn designed a house that, in addition to in-law quarters, has a large common room in the basement that has become a gathering place for their forty extended family members on special occasions. Thirteen years later, the entire family has been pleased with this arrangement. More recently, because Harold and Mary experienced some decline in their health, the family has decided to gather yearly, or as needed, to assess any changes that need to be addressed.

Option 7: Continuing care retirement community

Some of us enter a continuing care community to simplify our lives, to be in a social setting that is enriching, and to be assured of access to health care. These communities span a full range of housing choices, including condos, cottages, and apartments. The residents relate with peers in conversations and activities that are compatible with their stage of life. Most of these centers provide stimulating activities, lectures, and concerts. Many have recreational facilities such as indoor swimming pools, exercise rooms, woodworking shops, and hiking trails. People who choose these settings can find new purpose and support. They feel relieved that they no longer have to care for their home.

Dick and Ruth chose to downsize and move into a retirement community in their early seventies. Now that they have fewer housekeeping responsibilities and no property to maintain, they have more time to appreciate what is important to them: friends, reading, enjoying creation, and spending more time with their grandchildren. It also gives them satisfaction to realize that disposing of possessions and selling their property will not burden their children in the future. Nor will the children be responsible for their medical needs later in life.

Their children host most of the large family gatherings. However, they frequently share Sunday meals with Dick and Ruth in one of the campus dining rooms. Family holiday events can be held in a large community room with a kitchen, piano, and comfy upholstered furniture. The younger grandchildren quickly adapted to the new opportunities for play, including enjoying more space to ride bikes and scooters, a swimming pool, and a playground.

Perhaps the biggest attraction that these communities have is the availability of full-range health care, including in-home services in their cottage or apartment. When their health declines further, they may be admitted to intermediate, skilled care, or memory care units depending on their needs. This brings a sense of security to the residents and to their families. Regardless of the level of decline, it is important for adult children to continue to be involved with their parents and to not assume that all of their parents' needs will be met by the nursing staff.

One drawback for some people is that these continuing care communities lack age diversity and other aspects of the neighborhoods they used to live in. One author refers to these settings as "elder islands." Although residents have contact with the outside world when they leave campus or when their family visits, most of the time they are around people their own age. Retirement communities can be places of more sunsets than sunrises.

Option 8: Independent nursing care facility

Some nursing care facilities are stand-alone operations that only offer various levels of nursing and rehabilitation care. Some include memory care units. They have no cottages, condos, or apartments.

Many of their residents are transferred directly from a hospital following an acute medical crisis. Some receive physical therapy and are able to return home. Studies show that about 40 percent of us who are sixty-five and older will at some point have a short stay in a nursing care facility and be discharged to our homes or to the care of relatives.[3]

Many people who are admitted to these facilities have little chance of recovery. They may have suffered a debilitating stroke, have severe Parkinson's disease, or some form of dementia. Women over eighty-five with some level of dementia occupy the largest number of beds in long-term care. The average length of stay for people needing personal and skilled care is about two years.[4]

One common misunderstanding is that persons need to live in a continuing care community to be assured that they will have access to a nursing home bed when they need it. However, if they are living in their own home and are hospitalized for a serious illness that requires long-term care, the hospital social worker will find a bed—sometimes in an independent nursing care facility. All such facilities are regulated by state and federal agencies and must meet minimal standards for nursing care, nutrition, safety, and basic social needs.

As with most medical services, the architecture, aesthetics, and the environment in these facilities vary a great deal. Some are cheerful, attractive units with dedicated staff members. They have in-house activity programs that attempt to create a stimulating and compassionate environment. But many remain hospital-like facilities with long halls and large dining rooms.

After Millard had a stroke, his wife, Mary, cared for him at home for many years. When her health declined and she could no longer attend to him, they entered an independent nursing facility. Within weeks of arriving, Mary died unexpectedly, leaving Millard to adjust to life without her and to his new surroundings. Their daughter Lois was impressed with how quickly the staff rallied around her father to bring him comfort. They seemed to understand his needs, even though he couldn't speak after his stroke.

As he approached death, the family, including great-grandchildren who sat on his bed, gathered and sang with him as he breathed his last breath. The nurses washed his body, placed an embroidered white cloth over him, and escorted Millard and the family to the waiting funeral director. Lois is filled with gratitude for the countless ways the staff went beyond the call of duty to care for her parents.

Ending thoughts

Where we live is important to us. People who have experienced the numbing effects of homelessness or the insecurity
of being refugees long for a permanent home. Military or
professional families who move frequently can feel a loss
from not having a place to call their own. In the back of our
minds, we understand the earth to be a temporary home.
But it is natural that we desire some degree of stability for
where we live. Although the human spirit can be restless
and adventure-seeking, most of us eventually want to settle
down somewhere.

Where we are going to live and die weighs heavily on
most of us as we get older. It is difficult to think of giving
up our home place. Leaving portends a detachment from
neighbors, support systems, and possibly family at the time
when we need them most. So it is vital that we have many
conversations with our adult children and others about
where we will live.

Increasingly, institutions are becoming the place of
choice for our oldest members. While it may be necessary
for some of us to be in hospitals and nursing care facilities,
we need to explore all of the options that are available in
our communities before making a choice that has so much
importance.

Aging in place makes it possible to stay in our homes
near the people we care about most. However, the zoning
laws in some communities forbid families from adding on to
an existing house for aging parents to live in. That ignores
the large numbers of seniors who need housing, and the
expenses that come with caring for them in institutions. It
also overlooks the potential emotional and health benefits
to family units that are united during the aging process.

A good plan will include the input of all members and an equitable distribution of caregiving and costs. Most will want to have an attorney work out an understanding that promotes and protects all of the participants.

It is important to keep in mind that we are developing a family narrative that can be passed to future generations. Good alternatives exist. Families are writing new stories every day. Some involve regular and meaningful visits to parents in continuing care facilities. Some are about close ties between the generations, even though they live in separate locations. Other legacies are created when we live near each other or even in the same household. It is a conversation that we all need to have.

Thinking and Planning Ahead

1. Start the housing conversations early.

2. Know all of the options available.

3. Listen respectfully to parent's wishes.

4. Develop and implement the plan.

5. Are there any housing options you rule out? Why?

6. How will you resolve disagreements within the family?

7. If parent refuses to comply with the plan, how can you respond?

8. What is your role in supporting your parent's housing situation?

Conversations About Health

MOM: *I don't know why it is so hard to get my blood sugar down. The doctor said it's still over 200. He gave me a little lecture about being overweight and thinks I should set up an appointment with a dietitian. But I'm seventy-five, and maybe it doesn't matter anymore. My mom was a lot heavier than I am and had diabetes too. She lived until she was eighty-three. So maybe it's not such a big deal.*

DAD: *I think they make too much out of all these numbers. We know lots of people who are heavier than we are, and they seem to be doing okay. Sometimes I think doctors have to come up with things just to keep you coming back.*

DAUGHTER: *Mom just called and is upset about the lecture she got from the doctor. He's concerned about her weight and especially her diabetes. I told her that, from my experience as a nurse, bad things can happen when diabetes isn't controlled. At first, she got defensive and used the* old denial thing, like, "I don't eat much cake, and I'm not as heavy as my friends." But when I told her how much the grandchildren would miss her, she softened up and promised she would see the dietitian.

SON: *Good job! Glad that you can get through to her because I know I can't. My main worry is Dad. Did you know that he's had two fender-benders in the last three months? He says it was the other driver's fault, but that's not what the police report says. I know he doesn't see as well as he should, but he won't go to the eye doctor because he's afraid he has cataracts. Dad never did like the idea of going to the doctor, especially if he thought he'd have to have surgery.*

NIECE: *I don't know if it means anything to Aunt Polly when I visit her in the memory unit. She keeps asking me what my name is and can't carry on a conversation. She paces, looks tired, doesn't get anything out of living. She's been like this for over a year, and she's ninety now. But her daughter in Texas thinks the doctors should do everything they can to keep her alive. The staff at the unit thinks Polly should have signed an advance directive, but now it's too late. They should get in touch with her daughter.*

Many of us are in good health at the time of our retirement—and hopefully for a long time afterward. At first, we are able to remain active and enjoy our new life. Other than taking a few medications and being more careful when climbing ladders, we feel like not much has changed. So health and safety are not topics that are high on our list.

We do notice that our older friends are slowing down. Some even have serious illnesses. We worry a bit when we hear that 80 percent of us will develop a chronic medical condition and 50 percent of us will have several conditions at the same time.[1] We read the obituaries of people our age who are dying! If we know these people, these articles have a way of getting our attention. So it's not *whether* our health will decline but *when* and *how* it will happen. But, for the moment, we push those thoughts off for another day.

We take some comfort from knowing that advances in medicine can postpone the decline but are bothered by reports that most health care dollars in the United States are spent during the last few months of life. We pause and wonder if we will add to that number. Just knowing that the health care burden for people over eighty-five is six times higher than for people between fifty and fifty-four is troubling.[2] But for now, we have other problems to solve like finding enough guys for a foursome at the golf course.

Getting the conversation started

As much as we'd like to avoid the subject, beginning the conversation with our adult children, relatives, or friends who serve as our healthcare partners *before* problems develop is very important. With the help of our medical support team, we may be able to prevent some problems like diabetes, or at least keep them from getting worse. The conversations should also lead to choices that help us avoid accidents. An early start to these conversations enables our health care partners to become more effective in the ways they coach and support us. Although this thought doesn't seem urgent to us at the moment, it is important that we select one of our team members to become our health care agent just in case some unexpected medical problem develops. Though this person is our advocate while we are well, (s)he also makes medical decisions on our behalf when we can no longer speak for ourselves.

Unfortunately, many of us delay having these conversations until we are in a crisis. Our partners are then hampered by not knowing enough about our medical situation and may make choices for us that are not what we would have wanted. They may feel guilty for not asking to be involved earlier or resentful that we kept them out of the loop. Perhaps the greatest loss is that we missed having their emotional support and guidance to prevent the situation we are in. But we can do better. Let's get started!

Developing a medical file together

An early task of this partnership will be to create a medical file and to update it regularly. This file helps our healthcare partners to know more about our medical situation and to be better prepared to assist us. The file includes:

- A list of illnesses for which we are being treated, as well as allergies and past surgeries.
- A list of medications, including dosage instructions and possible side effects.
- Baseline numbers for blood pressure, cholesterol, glucose, and weight.
- Copies of signed consent forms permitting medical providers to release medical information to our healthcare partners.
- Appropriate legal documents about our health, including advance directives that spell out our wishes as we near death.
- The name and phone number of any healthcare proxy who has the legal authority to govern decision-making. The names, addresses, and phone

numbers for our healthcare providers and hospitals. (See Exhibits E and F.)

Partnering for prevention

As aging adults, there is much we can do to stay well for a longer time. To some extent, wellness is a choice. It can only be achieved through healthy lifestyle practices. Many of us ignore warning signs. One of the responsibilities of our healthcare partners is to gently nudge us into better choice-making. They can be more objective about what they are observing in our day-to-day living.

This partnership includes having them accompany us, at least some of the time, to doctors' visits. They are there to listen to what the doctor is saying and to interpret that information to us in the days ahead. They may ask clarifying questions, make notes, and remind us of what we need to do to remain healthy and safe. They can also provide important information to the doctor that we might not give.

To make it possible for our partners to get involved with our doctor, we need to sign a release form that permits sharing of health information. Many providers welcome having another set of ears and eyes to assist with the care of their patients. Our partner's role includes the monitoring and encouragement of our health and safety in the following ways:

Ensuring the proper use of medication

Most seniors are on medications to treat various conditions. Failure to take these medications as prescribed can have serious consequences. That problem can be minimized with the use of pill dispensers that guide us in knowing what medications are to be taken and when. Some pharmacists are willing to fill the pill dispensers weekly/biweekly/monthly (Some charge nominal fees while others may not). The healthcare partners can monitor our use of medications to determine if they are being taken correctly and to be vigilant for any side effects that might come from a medication.

In the United States, about 50 percent of us take five different medicines concurrently, while about 25 percent take between ten and nineteen medications.[3] Taking multiple medicines at the same time can be confusing and hazardous. When we have several prescribing doctors, it is vital that all members of the healthcare team know about the medications and supplements we are taking. Misuse of medication causes many unnecessary hospital admissions.

Jim's father had a debilitating stroke after taking twice the amount of an anticoagulant that he was prescribed. That happened because he was placed on a new medication that was a different color and strength. Jim regrets not paying more attention to his father's medications. Perhaps the stroke could have been prevented.

Encourage appropriate exercise

Following a daily exercise program may be one of the most important factors in maintaining our health in our senior years. The plan should include a year-round schedule that provides alternatives for bad weather. There are many good forms of exercise, including swimming and working out at a gym. Walking may be preferred because it is easy and inexpensive. Whatever exercise we choose should be discussed first with our doctor.

Regular exercise helps us maintain mobility, assists with balance, and increases muscle strength and bone health. It is also known to be beneficial for our heart and lung systems. Many of us are concerned about cognitive decline, and here too is another reason to maintain a fitness regimen for it is becoming evident that exercise is also important for brain and mental health. A study by the University of Illinois showed that three vigorous walks per week over a six-month period increased memory and reasoning ability.[4] The study suggests that the brain benefits from the increase in blood flow. Our health partners play a vital role in assuring that we continue some form of exercise.

Encourage weight control

It is estimated that 70 percent of seniors are overweight. That may come from our sedentary lifestyle and from a diet that is high in fat, sugar, and carbohydrates. Serving sizes have increased at home and in restaurants. In addition, snack foods, high-sugar drinks, and alcoholic beverages are readily available to us as we gather around our TV, movie theaters, and sports events.

An Oxford University study reveals that even moderately obese people are 50 percent more likely to die prematurely.[5] Moderately obese is usually defined as having a body mass index [BMI] of 30, and overweight is defined as having a BMI between 25 and 29.9. Obesity also contributes to type 2 diabetes, a serious illness that has doubled in the senior population over the past fifteen years. This can easily be noticed by the increased number of persons seen on motorized wheel chairs and in parking spaces for the handicapped. Although obesity is not always the cause, the number of seniors today who need knee and hip replacements is increasing. Because of joint and back pain, they often need medication to manage their symptoms. The impact of obesity on seniors cannot be overstated.

Encourage proper sleep patterns

Maintaining good sleep is important for keeping us well. Sleep experts say that we need between seven and eight hours of sleep each night. Inadequate sleep contributes to hypertension, mental confusion, anxiety, and depression. It can also make us less safe as drivers and interfere with our social relationships.

There are a number of reasons that we don't get enough sleep. There is evidence that our brain chemistry changes as we age, reducing the amount of melatonin, a brain chemical that we need for sleep. Some of us have sleep apnea, a condition in which the throat muscles weaken and interfere with breathing—sometimes causing hundreds of awakenings during the night. Sleep apnea can lead to significant medical, emotional, and marital problems. Remedies can include the use of a continuous positive airway pressure machine (CPAP) that assists with breathing or a snore guard made by a dentist that can help keep the air passages open.

Some of us simply have poor sleep because we drink caffeine products too late in the day or misuse alcohol. Eating large amounts of food before going to bed, engaging in highly stimulating activities, or being in situations that involve conflict also contribute to the problem. In addition, sleep can be difficult if we suffer from chronic pain or indigestion. Our medical team must be committed to helping us sleep well and to making wise choices if medication becomes necessary. Geriatrician Dr. Ken Brubaker considers controlled drugs like Ativan, Restoril, Sonata, and Ambien potentially harmful since they are commonly associated with frequent falls, especially during sleeping hours. Be sure to speak with your physician about the risks involved with any sleep-related medications.

Dental health

According to R. Todd Weaver, DMD, good dental health contributes to a longer and better quality of life. Studies show that gum disease can contribute to heart disease, diabetes, dementia, and other chronic illnesses when we fail to maintain good dental health. Loss of teeth prevents proper chewing of food, which in turn can create a choking hazard. Food that is not chewed adequately delays digestion and increases gastric reflux.

Our healthcare partners can make sure we receive regular dental care. If they provide transportation to the dentist, this allows them the opportunity to form a relationship with our dentist, making treatment decisions smoother and better informed. Because many of us are reluctant to spend money on dental care, adult children play a key role in making sure that finances are available for adequate care.

Eye health

Our vision may also be a cause for concern. Although many of us have worn glasses for a long time, some changes are now more troubling, including cataracts, macular degeneration, glaucoma, detached retinas, or other serious eye diseases. Poor vision can cause us to lose our drivers' license, make us more susceptible to falls, and make reading increasingly difficult. Vision losses can impede our social life and steal away esthetic pleasures like being able to see a sunset. Improved surgical procedures and medications can treat these conditions, but we may resist making a doctor's appointment because of denial or fear. In addition, some of these conditions come on gradually, and we may not recognize them until they can no longer be ignored. We should trust our healthcare partners to help us notice changes in our abilities, and we must be open to discussing safety precautions as well as treatment options.

Hearing loss

One of the most common health problems that many of us experience during our senior years is hearing loss. This happens to about two-thirds of us before we may be fully aware of it.[6] When we are approached about our hearing, we often minimize the problem or deny to ourselves that anybody even notices. We often blame others for not speaking loudly enough. Even though our hearing loss makes social interactions more difficult, many of us still resist getting hearing aids. We say they are uncomfortable to wear, hard to adjust to, and much too expensive. Vanity may be the biggest reason for not wearing hearing aids. It is important to face this loss because hearing is an important way to stay connected to those around us. When we can't hear well, we tend to disengage socially. That isn't good for our mental or physical health. We may need others to help us overcome our resistance to wearing hearing aids.

Mental health

Some of us enter our senior years with preexisting mental health challenges. Perhaps we are being treated for anxiety, depression, or other mental conditions. Most likely, we continue to be on medications that can keep us well. Some-times the doses need to be changed as we age, especially if we develop other medical problems.

Some of us may develop depression or anxiety *after* we retire. While that may come from physical losses, the cause may be from the absence of a daily routine. Retirement often brings with it less structure and a loss of purpose and identity. We can be affected by our reduced sense of independence, financial worries, and concerns about health. It is important to talk about our concerns with our spouse and adult children, friends, or a professional counselor. Our family doctor can also be helpful, especially in prescribing medications that can modify our moods.

To maintain good mental health, we need to discover new activities, hobbies, and a routine that brings meaning-ful structure into our lives. Giving to others through volun-teering may be the best medicine of all. Getting together regularly with friends can be enriching. Exercise is very important for mental health. These new activities can give us a reason to get up in the morning.

Preventing falls

During our senior years, more than a third of us experience a fall that causes an injury.[7] In fact, many of these falls lead to a hospital admission. Changes in balance, vision, and reduced strength increase the risk of an accident. Few of us make accurate assessments of our abilities and of the risks involved in daily activities. We need our healthcare partners to coach us when it comes to safety. They may observe hazards that we don't see.

We can reduce our risks by developing a healthy respect for height as we avoid ladders and refrain from climbing trees. We need to be especially careful on stairways and icy sidewalks and give special attention to uneven surfaces. Our healthcare partners can help us with a safety audit of our home. Safety audit assessment tools are readily available on the Internet. Occupational therapists can also assist with a safety audit; our physicians may be able to refer such a professional for us. Some of the changes may include rearranging the furniture to avoid tripping over chair legs, removing loose rugs, adding grab bars in the bathroom, and improving lighting.

Safe driving

One of our most significant safety risks—and most difficult to discuss—is driving. We and our caregivers don't want to think about our driving because it might mean giving up our license. That signals a loss of independence and a change in our identity. Perhaps more than any other loss, surrendering our car keys can be the most discouraging. Giving up driving may also mean that our caregivers will need to arrange transportation for us. What none of us can ignore, though, is the fact that seniors have an at-fault accident record that is second only to teen drivers.[8] There are some things that we can do to remain a safe driver:

- Drive more slowly.
- Allow more distance between our car and the car in front of us.
- Enter highways only where there are traffic lights, as much as possible.
- Avoid crossing two lanes when entering a highway, whenever possible.
- Avoid hazardous intersections.

- Drive when traffic volume is lower.
- Don't drive after dark or when tired.
- Avoid distractions from cell phones, interruptions from passengers, changing radio stations, or adjusting the air conditioning or heat.

Soon after retirement, it can be helpful for us to develop a written driving contract with our healthcare partners. The contract will spell out the conditions under which we should give up driving (see Exhibit G). A checklist can be an objective way to measure our safety on the road. AAA and AARP offer a safe driving evaluation for seniors. It does seem the older we are, the less objective we can be about our driving abilities. Hopefully, we will recognize the decline ourselves and voluntarily give up driving if we are at risk.

When George developed mild cognitive impairment, he talked with his doctor about not feeling safe on the road. He agreed to take a driving evaluation test, which he failed, and then he turned in his license. Although he felt the loss of independence, he and his family were relieved that the decision was made before he had an accident or became disoriented.

This early written agreement that we make with our partners gives them the freedom to ask for our keys and to sell our vehicle even if we don't recognize that our driving is becoming unsafe. Our partners' commitment to treat us with sensitivity and patience during this time of transition can help to reduce the emotional impact of our loss. Joining with our healthcare partners to plan for alternative arrangements is essential. It is important to recognize that our safety—and the safety of others—is at stake.

When Joe talked with his eighty-nine-year-old mother about giving up driving, he was surprised that she felt relieved to be free of the responsibility. She said, "You listened to me when you were young, and now I want to listen to you." Joe was grateful for her positive response.

Unfortunately, not all of us have a positive attitude about turning in the keys. That makes it especially painful for our caregivers. The older we are when we start these discussions, the more difficult it may be. We need to plan ahead, and we need to do our best to trust our caregivers and be willing to accept when the time comes to move over to the passenger seat.

Managing ongoing medical challenges

Although there is much that we can do to prevent or minimize illnesses and reduce accidents, some situations are past the point of prevention. This calls for aggressive management to prevent further losses. It also requires that we make adjustments that can improve our quality of life. Those of us who have conditions like diabetes, hypertension, arthritis, and heart disease will need aggressive management to prevent them from advancing. Various medications are available to help us control them. This may require changes in our lifestyle, including our diet and stress levels. We must be committed to regular exercise and physical therapy, if needed. Surgery might be indicated for joint problems. Some of us resist surgery because of fear or expense, even though it could be helpful in keeping us mobile and pain-free. We should discuss these concerns with our healthcare partners as well as our physicians, and we need to be open to their recommendations.

During this life stage, some of us will be diagnosed with cancer. The diagnosis fills us with fear. We don't look forward to invasive surgery, chemotherapy, or radiation. Even though some forms of this disease have good survival rates, others do not. Whatever our particular cancer may be, it will likely change our lives in a major way. It is even more important that our healthcare partners support us throughout the treatment process, including accompanying us to doctor visits. Their more objective presence helps us make the best decisions about treatment. They can play an important role in asking questions and hearing some details we miss. Together as partners, we then review what we heard and weigh the long-term benefits versus the immediate physical toll on our quality of life. Their support during this stressful time is very important.

Cognitive impairment

Perhaps the most dreaded aspect of aging is the loss of mental acuity. Although they come with different names (i.e.: Alzheimer's disease, Lewy body disease, vascular dementia, and so on), all forms of mental decline are profoundly disabling. They usually involve the loss of memory, recognition of place and person, self-care, communication, bodily functions, ambulation, and other abilities. In their early stages, these losses are clearly frightening and discouraging because seniors are still aware enough to know that something is wrong. In the later stages, seniors may not realize what is happening. These illnesses are wrenching for family and friends to observe.

Although research is revealing some of the causes of cognitive decline, little can be done at the present time to stop the progression of the disease once it reaches a certain point. However, before that point, the Rush Memory and Aging Project discovered that seniors with a high score on "purpose in life" were more than twice as likely to have avoided an Alzheimer's diagnosis. Among other things, the study emphasizes the importance of exercise, diet, and friendships in contributing to slower rates of cognitive decline. This is important economically and emotionally because it can shorten the length of time that seniors may need institutional care prior to their death.

Because more people are living into their eighties and beyond, it is likely that the number of seniors who have some form of memory loss will increase. The role of caregivers is to stay engaged, even when their loved one has difficulty with memory or communicating. The importance of being touched and comforted cannot be overstated. Family and friends can provide generous amounts of support to spouses and other caregivers.

Life at the end: Hard choices

Unless we die suddenly, the decline in our health will increase in severity and complexity as we age. We will need our family even more, and the earlier conversations we have had with each other will be even more important. It is difficult to know what to do when an illness has no remedy or when treatments carry a high risk. Our age, level of cognitive functioning, and the presence of other complicating conditions factor into the decisions we will make.

Some of these decisions may be quite difficult. If an orthopedist suggests surgery for an arthritic spine when we are sixty-eight but can't promise to completely resolve our pain, what should we do? If we are diagnosed with prostate cancer when we are seventy-five, should we proceed with treatment that produces ongoing side effects? If we are in our nineties and the cardiologist recommends a pacemaker, should we proceed even if we are showing signs of dementia?

Our caregivers should be our advocate when important questions are raised during our visits with various doctors. They can assist us in gathering the necessary information to help us better understand the potential for a significant recovery. Palliative care physician Dr. Tom Miller says that, when we are in a medical crisis, we often have multiple specialists attending us. Each may be offering options specific to their concerns. The caregivers should help the medical team understand what kind of life their loved one hopes to live and should ask questions about how likely each proposed treatment is able to achieve this. The caregiver should ask (or give permission) for the specialists to discuss openly the prognosis for recovery and for living the life that the patient will find meaningful. Though it may be difficult to hear and accept the facts, this information will be helpful in making decisions about their care.

When we are confronted with the reality of death, sometimes we and our caregivers can have second thoughts about the end-of-life choices we made earlier, especially our commitment to not artificially extend life when recovery is not possible. Death is never easy to face—for us or for those closest to us. We know temporary emotions can get in the way. But it is important to have our wishes respected, even if our family members have mixed feelings.

Mahlon developed an aggressive form of pseudobulbar palsy in his sixties and gradually lost his ability to care for himself. As the condition worsened, he had difficulty swallowing. The doctor recommended inserting a feeding tube to provide proper nutrition. Mahlon rejected that idea. The medical staff asked him three different times until they accepted his answer. His wife, Esther, and their children were at peace with the decision not to extend his life in this way. He had minimal quality of life, and death was a release for him when he passed away at age seventy. It was still a painful loss for the family, but they could take comfort in knowing they had respected his wishes.

Truman was seventy-nine years old and in serious decline from atypical Parkinson's disease when he developed meningitis and was hospitalized. When he didn't respond to the treatment, the attending doctor suggested he be flown to a teaching hospital across the mountains for more aggressive care. His wife, Betty, and their adult children were concerned about the quality of life for Truman and knew the experimental treatment was not what he would have wanted. Betty told the doctor, "This is one trip over the mountain that Truman will not have to make." He died peacefully several days later in the hospital.

Despite the fact that most of us say we want to die at home, many of us still seek care in hospitals. It is where we usually go when we are sick or injured, even when it is clear that we have little chance of recovery. However, the number of seniors dying in hospitals continues to decline from 80 percent in 1995 to around 24 percent at present. The number of persons dying in nursing home facilities has remained at about 21 percent. More of us are seeking hospice care at home or in hospice-care centers. The ability of hospice to offer palliative and end-stage care to the dying and to give emotional support to relatives is outstanding. Helping us accept death as a normal part of living can be invaluable.

It is necessary to appoint a person as our healthcare agent who is authorized to carry out our end-of-life wishes when we can no longer speak for ourselves. Our agent can present the appropriate papers to our attending doctor, permitting him/her to carry out our wishes not to receive any life-sustaining treatment if we so choose. However, if there is a family member who disagrees with this decision, the physician is caught in the middle and may not follow through with our wishes. Dr. Glenn Stoltzfus, a hospital-based physician, says that, in his experience, it is very important for the family to be united in supporting the end-of-life wishes of their loved one. Otherwise the papers are "only conversation starters." Family conflict may prolong the dying process and prevent family members from experiencing normal and healthy grieving.

If we are not in an emergency situation but have been given a terminal diagnosis, a palliative care physician can help us clarify our wishes for how we want to live in the time leading up to our death. Dr. David J. Casarett says it is very important that we have a conversation with our caregivers and our physician to ensure that our wishes are carried out. The decisions we make can give all of us more control, a greater sense of peace, and preserve the dignity of the dying person. He suggests that each of us answer the following questions:

- Where do we want to be when we die?
- With whom do we want to spend our remaining time?
- How do we want to spend the time that we are given?
- Are there any unsettled issues with family and friends that we want to resolve?
- How do we want to die?

Ending thoughts

In our early retirement years, many of us believe that we don't need help from anyone to prepare for what is ahead of us. But when unexpected challenges come, we realize that nothing in the previous years has prepared us for this life stage. Much as we would like to avoid thinking about it, our health will change. For some of us, it will come sooner, and for others, later. In the meantime, there is much we can do to manage our wellness. Choices about our lifestyle can be life-giving or life-losing. Good choice-making can contribute to a final life stage that is rich, vigorous, and filled with meaning.

Given the fact that none of us are experts on our own aging, we need the help of various team members, including our adult children, relatives, friends, and our medical team, to guide us in making wise choices. Health and safety are, to a large degree, a choice, especially in the earlier years. When the inevitable decline begins, our healthcare partners are there to offer guidance and support. None of us should experience decline and death alone. Our healthcare team can assist us in making choices about medical care and end-of-life wishes. Having the team with us from the beginning of our retirement years until the end provides the emotional support so important to all of us.

Thinking and Planning Ahead

1. Caregivers play an essential role in reinforcing preventive health strategies.

2. Managing treatment options requires a team approach.

3. Stating clearly our values and wishes for end-of-life care ensures a better outcome.

4. What approach should I use if I am concerned about my dad's driving?

5. Why is my mother so resistant to following through with her doctor's recommendations?

6. How can we support mother in her wish to care for dad at home? If we don't think she can manage everything, what compromises can we all agree to?

Left Behind

One experience: *I don't know whether it makes any difference if I visit my husband in the nursing home every day. He's so confused that I don't think he even recognizes me. In some ways, it seems like he has already died. He was diagnosed with Alzheimer's a few years ago, but I saw him slipping away long before that. It's so hard to see him in this condition. We had forty-eight very good years. He was bright and outgoing—and now this. But we made a sacred promise to each other, and I will do what I can to be with him to the end. I still love him—maybe now more than ever.*

Second experience: *When my wife died a year ago, I didn't know how hard it would be. We had no time to prepare for what happened. Neither of us knew that she had a heart condition, and her death took even the doctor by surprise. Now I wish we had talked about dying. There's so much I should have told her and so much we could have done together. But she was just seventy and seemed to be in good health. We took too much for granted. Now I have a hard time sleeping. I've lost twenty pounds. I know I'm only* *seventy-two and could get married again. But I can't bear the thought. My kids are telling me that I have to get out more, and they even hint that I should soon start dating. But not now—maybe never.*

Third experience: *I just wasn't prepared to have Dad die. I knew he had prostate cancer, but I didn't think it had spread. Besides, he was only sixty. He was helping me with some house projects, and it was fun to go fishing with him and my son. We had our problems when I was younger, but when I had children of my own, I was able to understand why parents have to say "no." It felt good to start getting to know him as an adult. And now he's gone! I know I can talk with my father-in-law, but it's not the same.*

The reality of being left behind

Earlier in our marriage, we didn't give much thought to losing our spouse, whether from a disabling disease, an injury, or from death. It's probably good that our focus was on other things. But now we can't escape these thoughts when we attend the funerals of people our age, or as we offer comfort to a friend whose spouse is in a nursing home. We can't ignore the despair we see in these people's eyes and begin to realize that it could happen to us. It is a reality that has become a part of our life.

These events make us more aware of the chest pains or memory lapses in our spouse. For a time, we are reassured when we get encouraging tests results from the doctor, and we pass these events off as a part of normal aging. But thoughts of life without them—the grief and the loneliness—become more common. We try to imagine what it would be like to attend events by ourselves, to eat alone, and to no longer have our companion to share our inner thoughts with. Few of us have had experience with such solitude, and we certainly don't look forward to gaining it this way.

Our adult children may first become confronted with thoughts of losing us when their friend loses a parent. Although the implications for adult children aren't the same as what a spouse might experience, our death, injury, or illness will change their lives as well. For some, it will mean providing more support to their surviving parent. For others, it means losing a special relationship that they had with each other. Some feel a particular loss because they had enjoyed seeing their children form a bond with the grandparent who died. The loss becomes more complicated if an adult child was in conflict with this parent and now will be unable to reconcile.

When we lose our spouse, it is never easy. We are left to grieve deeply and feel an overwhelming loneliness. It can be especially painful if the loss happens early in the senior years. At that point, we had been looking forward to spending stress-free time together, and now that hope is gone. The years ahead seem empty and without purpose for the survivor. If we are in our later years when the loss occurs, it can be challenging because we are more fragile and dependent on each other.

Left behind by chronic illness

The death of a spouse, though, is not the only way we can be left behind. When our spouse develops an incapacitating illness or has an accident that is disabling, we are left behind too. Not only have we lost their companionship, but now we are faced daily with their challenges. Elvin was diagnosed with multiple sclerosis when he was thirty-three years old. He and Roberta had been married eight years when he began showing some symptoms. Knowing that her husband would not get better, Roberta felt keenly the responsibility of raising their two young children alone, especially as the disease progressed and left him unable to communicate and wheelchair-bound. Although she faithfully honored her pledge to remain by his side, the thirty years that he was ill were filled with loneliness. The marriage that she had dreamed of on the day of her wedding was no longer possible. She gave him wonderful care and unlimited love, but in many respects, she was left behind. Family, friends, and professional caregivers gave her some assistance, but Roberta was in some ways already a widow.

Similar stories are told by persons confronted with situations in which their mates are disabled with crippling arthritis, incapacitated by strokes, or visited with multiple recurrences of cancer. Life revolves around trips to the doctor, surgery, radiation treatment, pain, side effects, and visiting the spouse in hospital rooms. The normal joys that were anticipated are set aside. When the spouse dies, it can be difficult for the survivor to rediscover a new purpose or identity. Some find meaning in their work, in new friendships, and some reach out in supportive ways to other persons who are faced with similar circumstances. Nonetheless, they continue to feel the pain of their lost relationship.

A feeling of abandonment can also arise when a spouse develops cognitive impairment. Early-onset Alzheimer's disease, a disabling brain condition that can show symptoms as early as age fifty, is particularly troubling. We experience profound grief knowing that our loved one is beginning to lose their ability to reason, remember, and relate to us. The body is alive but not the mind. We had been looking forward to many good years together in retirement. Now those hopes are shattered. Our memories are filled with the times that our spouse was with us at our children's school plays or as we sat together on lawn chairs at Little League games. Now they aren't able to go to our grandchildren's activities. Our wedding anniversaries slip by uneventfully, and we are left only with memories of the good times from the past.

Some other forms of cognitive impairment don't appear until later in life. Though these persons are older, families still feel helpless and sad when a loved one becomes impaired. Seth began showing signs of forgetfulness when he was in his seventies. This highly skilled craftsman had high standards for the cabinets and furniture he built. He was also diligent about finances and his checkbook. As his illness progressed, Seth found it more difficult to craft furniture to his satisfaction. He had trouble balancing his checkbook. At first, he blamed the bank for the accounting mistakes. His wife, Ginny, became more concerned when he had trouble handling the money for his class reunion, for which he served as treasurer, something he had done with precision for many years.

Seth was also aware that something was wrong. When he was still alert enough to ask Ginny about his confusion, she suggested that it could be dementia. It was as if he had already known and was relieved to have it acknowledged. His only request to her was, "Will you hang in there with me?"

It was not an easy decision for Ginny to move him from their cottage into skilled care at the continuing care community where they would spend the rest of their time together.

In the four years leading up to his death, he became profoundly incapacitated and was unable to communicate. Although she was occasionally comforted by a smile from Seth, Ginny was left behind by an illness that took her loving husband's spirit away. After his death, Ginny took comfort in knowing that she had kept her promise to "hang in there" with him. She experienced lots of times of stress and grief throughout the illness but is thankful for the ways her children and grandchildren offered help during Seth's decline.

Impact of parent's disability on adult children

While adult children experience our disability differently than we do, most are affected deeply by what they are witnessing. The parent who used to be strong, competent, and engaged is now becoming a shadow of their former self. The mother and father—who gave them life, who held them on their lap, came to their dance recitals and soccer games—are now unable to give much back. The giver has become the receiver. Parents need to recognize what this means to the adult child and to acknowledge to them how difficult this might be. Indeed, for many adult children, this is the first time they are faced with the responsibility of becoming a caregiver to a parent. This change is never easy, and for some, providing care may be impossible. Not offering care, though, can carry with it a burden of guilt. It can be helpful if families share these thoughts and feelings early—before the changes begin to happen.

Furthermore, when these changes begin, many adult children are in the midst of a demanding career. They may also be busy with the day-to-day needs of their own families and trying to find time to nurture their marriages. It won't take long to realize the toll that caregiving is having on them. The load becomes even heavier if they have no siblings or if they have siblings who are unable or unwilling to help. When the phone rings, they wonder if it is another request for help with balancing the checkbook. If mom is feeling chest pain, should the adult child cancel their plans to go to the company picnic even if the doctor assured her that she has a healthy heart? Or when dad falls in the bathroom at night, should the adult child get dressed and drive thirty miles to offer assistance?

When adult children are unable to offer direct care because of careers or other demands, they may need to seek substitute help for their parents for housekeeping, yard work, bookkeeping, and other practical needs. If moderate levels of medical care are needed, in-home healthcare agencies can perform these services. When their needs increase, it may be necessary for the parent to be admitted to a continuing care facility. Obviously, parents who are able to remain at home must be willing to have these services provided by other persons. If they refuse, it may be necessary for the family physician or a worker from the local agency on aging to intervene and implement a solution.

Adult children who are able to provide some level of care—even in small amounts—can experience a deep sense of satisfaction. In spite of making sacrifices, they accept their responsibility as an opportunity—not a burden—and find ways to balance career and family responsibilities with the needs of their parent. They are also comfortable accepting the services that others can provide, including institutional care. These decisions will be easier to make if all the family members have prepared in advance for the changes that are taking place.

Left behind by death

For some of us, the death of our spouse happens without warning early in our retirement years. Sometimes it occurs suddenly from an accident or unexpected medical crisis. Because we have no time to prepare, we are left numb and in grief. Many of us lose our spouse over a longer period of time. They may suffer from an incurable illness that doesn't cause an immediate death, such as cancer or chronic heart failure. Under those circumstances, death may be easier to accept because our spouse is in pain, sick, and confined to a hospital bed. Sometimes we may even welcome death. Some persons reject life-extending care when recovery is not possible but instead choose palliative and hospice care. Regardless of our choice, we are confronted with a deep sense of loss as we reflect on the good times we had together. Gone now is the companionship that we treasured for so many years.

After Edgar's wife, Gladys, died at age eighty, he wrote her the following:

When I woke up on Monday morning (April 12) . . . no, let's go back a few days. Remember? It was Saturday. We loaded our newspapers into the car and headed for Daniel's, your farmer friend. While I unloaded the papers, the children deposited the baby goat on your lap, dirty feet and all. You didn't seem to mind—you always enjoyed the kids. Then we headed across country in the direction of Manheim. We were not sure of the road, but the direction seemed right, and we enjoyed the ride. Farmers were working their fields, some with horses. Flowers and blossoming trees were in full bloom—not a cloud in the sky. Temperature— shirtsleeve-comfortable. I commented, "What a nice spring day." You said, "Maybe my last." We wiped a few tears and motored on.

Sunday, after lunch, I went for a long walk, and when I returned, I found a note saying that you had gone to visit Anita, who was recovering from a long illness. I probably watched some TV—you read. Then you remembered some bills that needed to be paid. It did not go well. I was afraid you would resign from tending our family finances, something you had done and done very well for years. After a bit you said, "The rest can wait—I am so tired—and confused."

We went to bed. I gave you the usual back rub. You thanked me, and we bade each other a good night. Then you appended, "I love you." I assured you that I loved you too—and so the day ended. Your last at 929 Broad Street.

Gladys suffered a stroke the next morning and died ten days later.

Impact on adult children from death of parent

The impact of the death of a parent on adult children will vary, depending on the circumstances. If we are seventy years old when we die, it will probably have a greater impact on our adult children than if we are one hundred. When the death happens suddenly and at a younger age, it is hard for them to prepare for the loss. This loss alerts them to the fact that their surviving parent now needs support and care. Seeing the grief of the surviving parent can be hard for an adult child to face. When adult children lose the second parent, they can experience an increased feeling of aloneness and a recognition that an era has come to an end. Perhaps, most of all, the loss of parents can awaken an awareness of their own mortality. The family in which they were raised now exists only in memory, through relationships with siblings and perhaps extended family.

Preparing for being alone

An important part of preparing for being alone is for spouses to live openly with each other and to maintain a transparent, compassionate, and loving relationship. We don't want to enter our senior years with unsettled conflict. We want to live—and die—without anything hidden or unresolved. It is important that we deal with these issues early in our senior years before we develop an illness that impairs our minds or before we die. Then, it is too late to apologize, forgive, explain, or to clear up any doubts. Too many survivors are left behind with "if only" thoughts. It is tragic to face the end of our life with unfinished conversations. In a similar way, we must choose to make peace with our adult children while we are still able.

When we are at peace with our spouse and our family, we are in a position to do as Sandy's family did as he lay dying from cancer. His children and grandchildren gathered at his bedside. In the midst of their tears, they were able to bless each other and reflect on memories from their past, knowing that his life was coming to a close. This memory will have an influence on shaping their lives in the years to come.

Early family conversations about our deaths

Just as parents and adult children need to talk about and plan for aging, they also need to talk about and plan for dying. There may be nothing else in our lives that we need to be more prepared for. The conversation about death might seem remote when we first bring it up, but we can approach the subject as a natural part of life—not a separate event. We must set aside any aversion to talking openly about it. We will even need to find ways of discussing death with our grandchildren. Often, young children will have already lost a favorite pet and can transpose some of that understanding to the loss of grandparents. Of course, timing and choosing words that are appropriate to the age of the grandchildren are important. Families who don't face death openly often experience more stress and conflict when death comes. The stories of family conflict around the time of death are legendary. That pain can be prevented.

Planning our memorial services

When we die, most of us choose to have a formal service to reflect on the meaning of our lives and to bring comfort to our family and friends. Early in our senior years, we should begin talking with our spouse and our adult children about some of our wishes for this service. It is helpful to list favorite texts, songs, and poems,and to identify who we might want to participate in the service. Obviously, if we live for a long time, those choices may need to be adjusted along the way.

The ways families plan the memorial service often reflect how they faced other important matters over the years. If they have been open and transparent, it is most likely that they will be so when planning a memorial service. Daryl and Lila established a pattern of openness with their family over a long period of time. So, after Daryl died at age eighty-two, the family was able to plan effectively for his memorial service. It not only reflected his wishes for the service but also their commitment to honor him in a quiet, reflective way that represented him as a warm, humble, and caring spiritual being. The family chose to structure the service in a way that guided speakers on both length and focus of their presentation. Expressions of grief were a part of the service. The music, reflections, prayers, and tributes allowed attenders to be enriched by the authenticity in the way he and his family had faced his life and death.

Increasingly though, the memorial service is referred to as a "celebration of life." Could this euphemistic language be an attempt to minimize our loss and grief? Perhaps we are more comfortable with gatherings of celebrations than we are with those that are about sadness and losses. Do we want to reshape this event in a way that minimizes the loss, so we can quickly return to our normal lives? Of course, a respectful amount of honoring the life of the deceased is appropriate and a source of comfort to the family. However, trying to reframe the loss in a way that minimizes its importance serves no one well.

Funeral plans that we made earlier should be seen only as a guide and should not restrict the thoughts and feelings of the adult children or surviving parent when they gather to plan the service. This may be the first time the children are stepping into a position of leadership with their surviving parent, and their ideas should be considered respectfully. Obviously, few of us have experience with planning a memorial service, and emotions can shape it in ways that may not have much positive meaning to the people who are attending. Planning ahead prevents families from having to make decisions about the service in the midst of grief.

Decisions about burial

The choices for how to dispose of the body have become more varied in recent years. Many families want an alternative to an expensive casket and large displays of flowers. Some churches now make simple wooden caskets available to their members, reflecting a spirit of simplicity and ecological sensitivity. Some families have found the experience of making a casket together to be a healing time. For five hundred years, religious groups like the Quakers have been preparing the body for burial in a shroud.

An increasing number of persons are choosing cremation, after which the remains are buried or scattered, depending on the preferences of the family. Family members may have differing views about cremation, based on religious convictions or personal preferences. There may be some value in having close relatives—including grandchildren—view the body of the deceased prior to burial or cremation. Sometimes families gather at the bedside at the time of death to say their goodbyes. Some persons choose to donate their bodies to medical science. John was surprised when his mother—then ninety-one—wanted to talk with him about doing just that. She was not feeling good about spending a lot of money for her funeral and now wanted to do something that might help other people.

Grieving

Moments of humor and storytelling can lighten grief, but they should not be used to cover feelings of loss. The human spirit needs to cry and grieve. To say that a funeral brings closure suggests a clinical fantasy more than reality. The idea that the family will neatly find its way through the various "stages of grief" seems offensive.

Those theories may work in a textbook but not usually in the real world.

With such a great diversity of human experience, it is simplistic to suggest that everyone will follow the same grieving script. When a parent has been ill for a long time, the family has already grieved and may even feel a sense of relief when their loved one dies. Greg and his siblings expressed just that at their father's funeral. They reflected on having lost their father some ten years earlier when his dementia robbed him of his ability to relate to them. By the time of his memorial service, they were free to share some of the good memories they had of their father.

New realities after the funeral

In the weeks and months following the funeral, the surviving spouse and adult children are faced with new realities. Hopefully, these challenges had been a part of earlier discussions they all had together. Ideally, the plan includes details about finances. Will the surviving spouse have enough money to live on as a single person? Are they competent to pay bills, balance the checkbook, and handle other financial details? If not, the family needs to find a skillful and trustworthy person to manage this.

Another decision confronting the family is where the surviving parent will live. Should they stay where they are if their health is good? Losing a spouse and a home at the same time can be difficult. Depending on the circumstances, it can be helpful to have an adult child stay with the parent during the night for a while. Some survivors occasionally take in boarders to provide some income and support.

The surviving spouse should be prepared to move if it is not safe to live alone or if they can't maintain or afford the property. The move may be to a smaller house, apartment, to a retirement community, or to live with one of the adult children. Having had earlier conversa tions with them about these options can make decisions easier now.

The spouse who wants to live independently should be able to handle daily living needs. Do they know how to cook and clean, launder, manage the property, and care for the car and personal health? Although a parent can get some support from adult children or from others for these tasks—especially during the early to middle senior years—having these skills is essential for maintaining independence. If parents allow themselves to become dependent on others prematurely, they will likely age more rapidly, experience reduced quality of life, and may be placed in institutional care earlier than expected.

It will be important for the survivor to establish a new independent life. It may be uncomfortable because it now happens as an individual—they are no longer a wife or husband. The survivor's identity has changed. They become aware quickly that they are a single person in a married world and find themselves reaching out to other survivors for companionship and socialization. Although they might turn to adult children for advice, more of the decisions now rest on the survivor.

It's important to develop new personal interests—per haps by volunteering or joining new groups. Some people may find it easier to develop a social life when they live in a retirement community. Adult children can play a role in providing companionship, but they can't be a permanent replacement for friendships and social activities. It's not fair to them, and it can also limit the survivor's involve ment with others.

Remarriage

Although most survivors remain single, some choose to remarry. Remarriage should always be discussed with adult children. When adult children believe that their parent isn't fully competent, they should express their reservations about the relationship to their parent. If the parent persists in their plans, adult children may need to talk with the family doctor, clergy, friends, other relatives, or even to a lawyer. Remarriages that are unwise need to be evaluated and confronted.

The following points are important to think about before considering remarriage:

- The survivor's age and the age of the potential spouse.
- How soon after the death of the original spouse the survivor begins to date.
- The survivor's emotional and physical health and that of the potential spouse.
- Religious and cultural differences.
- The relationship between adult children and potential stepparent.
- Financial arrangements.

When Richard's father, then in his late eighties, announced that he was going to marry for the third time, Richard and his siblings were very concerned. Their father hadn't done well in his first marriage when he was married to their mother. He was very controlling and eventually divorced her. His second marriage lasted fifty years because, as Richard described his stepmother, "she stood her ground" on many of their decisions despite the fact that he still attempted to control her.

When he told his adult children of his intention to marry a third time, he assured them that he and his wife-to-be had met with a lawyer and signed a prenuptial agreement. They were told that his assets would be passed on to them after he died. However, after his death, they learned that he hadn't been truthful and that, in fact, there was no prenuptial agreement. All of the assets were transferred to his wife who passed them on to her son. Richard and his siblings were left only with the responsibility of disposing of the contents of their father's home.

It is vital that the surviving parent and adult children talk about any potential remarriage before that parent begins entering a new relationship. No one wants their parent to make an impulsive decision based on loneliness or dependency. Emotions may lead parents into remarriage before they are ready. The parent may rationalize that they are making the right decision because of their mature age and life experience while others simply don't want to be a burden to their adult children.

While remarriage can be rich and meaningful—and sometimes even better than one's earlier union—it can also be complicated. It usually brings with it separate sets of adult children and grandchildren, plus family histories and rituals that are quite varied. These differences can be hard to adjust to, especially if family members are still grieving the loss of their loved one. It can be a challenge to know how to honor the memory of an original spouse while giving full love and commitment to the new spouse. Problems can also arise if one spouse brings a very different financial situation, including debt, into a marriage. Or one spouse may bring greater financial assets with them. A prenuptial agreement can ensure that all family members are treated fairly and that the best decisions are being made.

Many people do find fresh purpose in their new marriage. It can be life-giving—sometimes literally bringing physical, emotional, and spiritual health. This may happen especially for those who had given long-term care to a previous spouse. The new relationship can allow a couple to become active and reengaged with life. If it is a compatible marriage, the adult children and grandchildren can celebrate the new union and may even feel less responsibility to support their parent.

Mike and Karen entered their second marriage when they were in their mid-sixties. Mike had lost his first wife after a long battle with cancer. They had had a close relationship through forty-three years of marriage. They had lived in a number of different communities because Mike was a pastor. His wife was very supportive of him. When she was first diagnosed with cancer, she and Mike were optimistic about her chance of recovery. After some recurrences, it became clear that she would not live. They grieved deeply in the months leading up to her death. Their four children and several young grandchildren also were deeply affected by her death.

Karen's husband, a college professor, was killed instantly in a car accident when she was fifty-nine. Even though they loved each other, they were both busy with their careers and didn't talk much together—especially about the future. Karen was not prepared for this moment. Her grief was great, but the shock was even greater. As a relatively young widow, she was left to deal with details that she found overwhelming. Their two young adult children were just establishing their own homes in other states and were also deeply affected by the tragedy.

Mike and Karen and their families had known each other for many years before their spouses died. Since

Karen's husband had died some years earlier, she sent condolences to Mike when she heard of his wife's death. That contact eventually opened the door to a new friendship. They soon talked with their children about their budding relationship.

Although the adult children had no wish to blend the two sets of siblings together, they all supported the new marriage. The families celebrate holidays separately, partly because of the complexities in the number of persons involved and possibly to maintain some identity with their deceased parent. The grandchildren find it natural to relate to their new grandparents since they are the only ones that they have known.

Mike and Karen find it easy to have open communication with each other and often talk about the future. They feel comforted that they are able to talk about their previous spouses with each other and with their children. That preserves their memories while, at the same time, giving them freedom to celebrate their new life together. They signed a prenuptial agreement to ensure fair distribution of the assets to the adult children that they each brought into the marriage. Sharing this information with their families removed any mystery and possible future resentment about the wills.

Ending thoughts

We all know that someday we may lose our spouse—either to death or to a significant disability. It is especially important to accept that reality at the beginning of our senior years. It compels us to talk about the inevitable. The discussion doesn't need to be morbid or create an unnecessary sense of gloom. Indeed, openness about this subject brings a degree of comfort that frees us to enjoy our relationship even more.

We do each other a favor, too, by talking with our adult children or other caregivers about our future. We should discuss various possibilities that typically occur as we age—especially severe disability and death—and how our adult children can be helpful when this loss occurs.

However, none of us can ever fully prepare for the loss, grief, and helplessness we experience when a spouse or parent becomes disabled or dies. Talking about it earlier may help us face the loss with more preparedness, but the emotions that sweep over us can still be wrenching. For the surviving spouse, seeing the empty chair at the dinner table is painful, and sleeping alone can be difficult. We and our adult children are really left behind. Although we may find comfort in our memories, we need friends and family to provide support during this time of emptiness. We carry the burden together, and we heal together. Life can go on. We can find our way to a new place. We need all of our partners to help us get there.

Thinking and Planning Ahead

1. The loss of a spouse, whether through a disability or death, is profound and our recovery can be challenging.

2. Loss of a spouse/parent through death is less painful if conflict we had with them has been resolved.

3. Planning ahead with our family members for our memorial service brings a sense of comfort.

4. If we are thinking about remarrying, it is important to talk with our adult children before a new relationship begins and to honor their concerns.

5. How is a living death from a long-term illness different from a final death?

6. If adult children or their parents aren't able to talk about end-of-life issues, what might be done to help overcome their resistance?

7. If there is a difference of opinion regarding the funeral and disposal of the body, how can a family work to resolve these differences?

8. How can family members find new life together after the death of their loved one?

A Legacy of Family Conversations

On Halloween 2013, Stuart Farber, MD, experienced chest pain and shortness of breath and went to an emergency room for care. That began what he called "an odyssey with acute myelogenous leukemia" leading to his death on February 27, 2015. In his article, "Living Every Minute," published posthumously in the April 2015 *Journal of Pain and Symptom Management,* he reveals how he boldly faced his death (as well as the death of his wife who had a similar diagnosis shortly after his). He lamented, though, that he was caught up in a healthcare system that he believed to be based on the "medicalization of our lives" as he awaited his death.

In spite of being caught up in that system, he said "one of the most meaningful lessons that I have learned in the past year is the power of legacy." Faced with overwhelming anxiety about dying, he also discovered that the anxiety came mainly from the fear that he "would not be able to share with my family and community how much

I loved them and what I valued in our relationships . . . and that all our mutual loving and caring would be lost and forgotten."

Responding to this insight, he wrote letters to his wife, sons, and grandchildren "sharing my love, acknowledging their gifts, and describing my hopes for them." He then wrote songs for them to play at his wake. These choices brought him a great sense of calm, but he admits that "this is something I should have been doing all my life and not as I sit on the brink of mortality."

A legacy of mutual loving and caring is something all of us should be thinking about throughout our lives. Our acts and our words convey unmistakably who we are and how we value the people around us. We want to be remembered as persons who were transparent, loving, honoring, humble, confessing, and forgiving. Our legacy will be shaped by our acts, deeds, and words. But as Dr. Farber suggests, those closest to us should not have to wait until they are sitting by our bedside as we near death to hear words of affirmation for the first time. At any point, a life-changing accident, medical event, or cognitive loss may make it impossible to convey our love to those around us.

Another important part of our legacy is revealed through the ways we adjust to aging. When we retire, we leave behind a lifetime of work, an identity, and a focused purpose. To some extent what we *did* for our work was who we *were*. Now, our legacy is shaped by how we handle the losses we experience as we age. Some of us accept these losses gracefully as a part of the normal cycle of life and death. Some are angry and resentful. Others simply give up and passively wait for the end to come. Of course, our overall health, including the health of our brain, may play an important part in how we handle the changes.

One of the most necessary conversations we need to have with family and friends is about the losses we are experiencing. Many of us suffer in silence and deprive ourselves receiving support from our loved ones. Conversations with family and friends can bring a degree of comfort and new hope that enriches our lives—and theirs. Our adjustment to these changes is being observed by our children, grandchildren, and by those around us. The rewards are bountiful when we partner with our family and friends throughout our life. This too is a part of our legacy.

Legacies vary a great deal from person to person. They reflect our personalities, life circumstances, and our systems of belief. All are important in their own way. The following are stories of families that demonstrate choices that enrich their legacies.

Finding a new purpose

Jeff and Margaret are retired professionals in their sixties and active as volunteers. Jeff sold his share of his business at age sixty, something he'd begun planning in his forties. Jeff and Margaret had careers independent from each other and looked forward to finding ways to work together in their retirement years.

When looking at their retirement, Jeff and Margaret set some goals for travel and service. These goals would be difficult to meet if they continued to live in their large home. Realizing this, they chose to downsize and move to a condominium community. They were able to pass on the family "stuff." It was rewarding to see their adult children and grandchildren enjoy these things and put them to practical use.

Some advantages of condo living for Jeff and Margaret include the freedom to help others, whether it is their
children, community, or faith-based service projects. This
freedom also makes it more possible to travel. In addition,
they find they enjoy the community life that condo living
provides.

They are passionate about reaching out to those around
them who may not have family support. One way they've
done this is by purchasing a rental property for a single
friend with no immediate family. It is a pattern they learned
from the generation before them and are gratified to see
their children doing some of the same things. Jeff's and
Margaret's actions are an important part of the conversations they have with their family. And they have a broader
view of who is considered family.

Earlier in his life, Jeff helped his widowed mother make
many decisions as she began to decline in health. Decisions
about where to live and when to stop driving were easier
because they had begun those conversations earlier. Jeff
tried to be sensitive to his mother's losses and fortunately
didn't have to make any decisions in a crisis. Surely that
experience helped to shape his thoughts as he and Margaret
made preparations for themselves.

Jeff and Margaret laugh when they remember how
they wrestled with the decision to downsize. They worried whether family time would happen in a smaller place
with a smaller yard. They now realize family time does not
depend on where you live. Without many of the repetitive
tasks required to keep up a large house and property, they
have the freedom to make time for the people and things
important in their lives.

They have benefited by not having the expenses of the
large property, allowing for more discretionary income.

Jeff and Margaret communicate well as they continue to make decisions in these years of retirement. Being proactive about preparing for the changes in their lives has been freeing for them.

Building three-generational relationships

As children, Charity and her husband Steve both lived in countries where three-generational living was common. They were impressed by how natural this seemed to be. Now in their thirties, they wanted their sons to come to know what they witnessed as children. While Charity was finishing her training to become a registered nurse, she talked with her parents, Jim and Donna, about this dream. She emphasized what it would mean to the children and also how important it would be to her to be able to care for her parents when they were old. Both Jim and Donna responded with enthusiasm and suggested that they begin planning to allow them to be with the boys while they were still young and before Jim and Donna were old!

The next months were filled with dreaming—and planning. Eventually they found a property that, with some renovations, would provide private space for both families as well as many opportunities to be together. As the plans progressed, there were some challenges to overcome. To their surprise, their homes sold quickly but before the renovations were completed on the new house. During that time, Charity gave birth to their third son. They were all amazed at how smooth the transition was during the months that they shared space before the renovations were completed. However, a surprise that none of them could be prepared for was when Donna was diagnosed with cancer as they were each settling into their new spaces.

They were all surrounded by friends and extended family during the months of Donna's surgery and treatment. Being in the same house made it possible for Charity to provide some care to her mother while preserving some energy for her own children. She is grateful that she didn't have to spend time on the road, going to care for her mother at her former home. The boys did have some adjustment reactions during the early months after the move, including getting used to a new baby, their mother's new part-time job, their grandmother's cancer, and becoming accustomed to their new home. After the remodeling was finished and Jim and Donna moved into their own space, Steve said it kind of felt like a divorce. Charity and Steve especially missed having their parents around to maintain a clean kitchen!

Steve loves the new, larger property where he can expand his passion for gardening. His young sons are learning important lessons as they work side by side with him and have opportunities to explore the outdoors. He is grateful to have his in-laws around to share the maintenance responsibilities and appreciates the constructive ways that they interact with the grandchildren—perhaps filling a void he experienced as a child. He knew Jim was fully engaged when he cleared a trail in the woods after a heavy snow so the children and their friends could sled safely.

Donna found that holding her new grandchild gave her much joy and comfort during the months of her treatment. She experienced hope and new life when looking into his eyes. There were occasions when she needed more quiet time, and the older boys seemed to understand. They were somewhat traumatized earlier to see how fragile she looked when they visited her in the hospital. They told Donna that they didn't want her to lose her hair but were able to adjust when it did happen. They are more comfortable, though, when she wears her wig. She and Jim cherish reading bedtime stories to the boys.

Jim is surprised by how much pleasure he is getting from mowing the lawn and doing other outside chores. He had considered mowing his former yard an intrusion to his busy work schedule. Involving the two older boys in his tasks is rewarding. Each Monday, they take turns loading the trash onto the trailer and ride with him on the tractor to the bottom of the hill where it is picked up by the trash men. The boys often appear at Grandpa's kitchen on Saturday, eager to help make pancakes. They proudly take a plateful back to their kitchen to share with their parents.

Jim and Donna had expected to keep the door closed between the households but find it is open most of the time. They never tire of seeing the bright eyes of anticipation from the grandchildren as they interact with them. Charity, Steve, Donna, and Jim have become more aware of the fragility of life and an uncertain future. They are grateful for whatever time they may have with each other. They sense that even the grandchildren are absorbing the beauty of living each day to its fullest. They are building memories and a legacy together.

Estate-planning conversations

When Ben and Sue turned seventy, they decided to break with the pattern of secrecy about finances and other personal matters that was modeled by their parents and many in that generation. They felt the time had come to provide full disclosure of their finances and estate plans with their children *now* while they were of clear mind and in good health. Because of their gratitude for the amount of accumulated assets that they achieved, they wanted to be generous in what they gave to faith-based causes and, at the same time, be sensitive to the needs and feelings of their family.

Ben and Sue's goal was to present their estate to the children in a clear, straightforward way that would be understandable and easily accessed. They didn't want to leave a mess of undocumented assets in hard-to-find places with minimal indications of what their wishes were regarding the estate. Another goal was to convey a spirit of fairness to the children in hopes of avoiding any family conflict over their desire to distribute a significant portion of their assets to charity. One favorable factor was that, over the years, their children understood and had observed their faith priorities, tithing, economic understanding, and financial practices.

After meeting with a foundation representative from their denomination to explore all the options, Ben and Sue felt ready to call a family meeting to discuss their estate planning, to give full disclosure of their assets, and to share more about how they arrived at their decisions. Their plan was to "make haste slowly." When they told their adult children that they were updating their wills and wanted their participation, the children weren't interested. Ben and Sue realized, as parents, they would need to gently but purposely engage their children. Later, when they proposed a family meeting to discuss their estate planning, the children agreed to meet as they had more than a passing interest in various investment properties—especially favorite lake cottages. However, they had no knowledge about the value of the securities and retirement portfolios.

Prior to the first meeting, the children were sent information outlining what would be discussed as well as a financial statement and a document outlining options for estate distribution. Advanced information may seem a bit formal, but it helped reduce pre-meeting anxiety. As might be expected, the three children were surprised by what they learned, and each responded differently to the information. Because one of the children is single, they all agreed that only the three siblings (no in-laws) would attend the meetings. The siblings continued to have varying attitudes, concerns, and differences throughout the process.

At the first meeting, Ben and Sue began by sharing their death and burial plans, hoping to demonstrate that they were comfortable talking about these and other sensitive matters. Next on the agenda was the distribution of heirlooms and personal and physical properties. Wanting to avoid painful conflict, Ben and Sue prepared an inventory of all items of value and asked the children to offer ideas about how these things could be distributed. The pros and cons of their ideas were discussed. The third item was where the parents would live and who would take care of them when they could no longer care for themselves. Since health or infirmity was not an immediate issue, they agreed to revisit this every few years.

Powers of attorney, durable powers of attorney for health care, living wills, executors, etc., were the fourth items on the agenda. After a full explanation of these terms, the children quickly volunteered according to their interests and abilities. The fifth item to discuss was the distribution of assets. Not surprisingly, the children expressed divergent views. Not achieving a consensus, Ben and Sue agreed to further consideration and to look at other options. However, they stated that any plan must honor their spiritual commitment to share fairly their assets with others as well as with their family. They did however agree to reserve the cottages for the children and grandchildren.

A second family meeting a year later focused on the plan to distribute assets other than the cottages and personal physical property to their family through a charitable remainder trust. The grandchildren would each receive a nominal cash distribution, and adult children would receive a percentage of the distribution from the corpus of the estate for a period of years, after which the corpus would become an endowed scholarship fund for students planning to enter church service positions. With this option, the children would receive approximately the same amount given to charity. The children accepted the charitable remainder trust proposal with mixed levels of support but without objecting. Previous items from the first meeting were reviewed, clarified, and adjusted as needed.

After finalizing all the necessary documents, a third meeting to include spouses was scheduled. Copies of wills, trusts, and the charitable remainder trust were shared, allowing time for clarifications. The location of the original legal documents, along with contact information, was also disclosed.

Each family meeting became more relaxed and informal. By the fourth meeting, there was no advance agenda or minutes. The family gathered around the table on the deck at the cottage for informal discussions, answering questions, providing clarifications, and doing some family planning not related particularly to estate matters. Ben and Sue cherish their family and the special times at the cottage and the process of working through the estate with their children. They know that family harmony and planning doesn't happen by accident but that it needs to be deliberate. They have a feeling of satisfaction from taking the lead to involve their children in their end-of-life planning.

Their children seemed to appreciate that their parents were trying to leave no surprises for them to sort out. While they didn't fully agree with the charitable remainder trust and the parents' benevolence, they didn't object or make disparaging remarks. All were in good spirits, accepting and appreciative of the opportunity to participate in the process and to better understand their parents' beliefs and values. Family meetings are still periodically called just to reflect and consider matters of importance.

Conversations through actions

Jonathan and Ada Martin, members of the Old Order Mennonite church, welcomed us warmly into their simple apartment. It is attached to the main house where their son, daughter-in-law, and eight children live. In their church community, it is common for extended families to live near each other. Even though five of their adult children have moved to different states in search of more affordable land, three remain in the home community.

Soon after we had settled into our chairs in the Martins' home, their grandchildren began to enter the room. They quietly took seats and listened carefully to what was being said. Later, their mother joined us, carrying a newborn child. One of the grandchildren was sent outside to find out when the father and sixteen-year-old brother would be coming in from the barn.

It is obvious that this family is committed to remaining tightly connected to each other in the cycle from birth to death. Although members of this faith tradition tend to converse more with actions than with words, when they do speak, their words carry importance. These traditions help their faith and their way of living to be passed on.

Because of the strong family and church connections, they don't depend on government agencies to provide care for their elderly. They talk relatively little about the changes that come with aging. Their traditions and ways of living are a kind of conversation.

Their commitments are also seen in the ways they share their compassion with others who aren't a part of their church. Ada's parents offered significant care to an "English" neighbor who developed a terminal illness. Later, when Ada's parents moved to a new community, the neighbor's husband, then a widower, asked to move along with them. He lived in a trailer behind their house and ate his meals with them. They cared for him until his death. As Ada was telling this story, the grandchildren paid close attention. Clearly the idea of caring for family, and even for "English" neighbors, was being imprinted on their young minds.

Modeling caregiving

Karen and Paul have three adult daughters and have fourteen grandchildren. Paul was a compassionate and competent staff technologist in the Imaging Department at a local hospital. Karen was a nurse supervisor in the same hospital for many years. She is a caring, compassionate, and competent person. Perhaps these qualities made it natural for her to respond to the needs of several of her family members over the years.

The most intense caregiving was that which she gave when her mother was diagnosed with cancer at age fifty-seven. Karen was then thirty-two. She took her mother for chemotherapy and supported her in many other ways until her death ten years later. During that time, Karen's father needed emotional and practical support. Although he ate many of his meals in a nearby restaurant, she would occasionally invite him to join her family for dinner. In addition, she assisted in obtaining a housekeeper for him. Later, when he showed some signs of confusion, she arranged for his admission to a continuing care community. Until his death ten years later, she and her husband Paul visited him frequently, took him to doctor's appointments, and brought him to family activities.

During this same time period, Karen and Paul provided support to three widowed aunts. None of them had relatives in the community. When two of these aunts came to the continuing care community where her father was living, Karen and Paul joined all of them once a week for a meal and a card game. Karen kept in touch regularly with another aunt who was in a similar facility and would occasionally be called by her nurse if there was a problem. Karen and Paul provided both emotional and practical support to all of these aging relatives.

Shortly after the death of her father, Paul needed to have both of his knees replaced. Unfortunately, he developed an autoimmune reaction to the surgery. It took a long time for the doctors to arrive at a diagnosis and to then find medication to control his symptoms. This was a very stressful time for both of them. Even though Paul's health has since stabilized, his level of physical activity and social interactions are limited. He and Karen realize his quality of life may never be fully restored. However, what they have come to value most is just being together. Earlier in their marriage, they had a marital crisis that could have ended their relationship but took important steps to restore their marriage. From that crisis, they learned to not take their marriage—or each other—for granted. As a part of their gratitude, they reach out to support other couples who are in marital crises.

Over the years, Karen and Paul have been deeply involved with their children and grandchildren. Karen would like to do more but is trying to find a balance in her own life. Paul encourages her to set boundaries. When a daughter offered to host a family dinner for a recent holiday, it wasn't easy for Karen to step out of her usual mother role. But when she did, and the day turned out well, it was an experience of celebration for everyone. Karen and Paul realized that, by accepting their daughter's invitation, they are now offering the *gift of caregiving* to the next generation. That, too, is a part of their legacy.

When reflecting on their caregiving, they acknowledge feeling overwhelmed at times and occasionally wanting to escape by moving far away. They wondered if they were making too many sacrifices to meet the needs of others. They truly were "sandwiched" between the generations. On balance though, they know that the rewards they experience from caregiving are greater than the struggles. Giving care to others is meaningful and not a burden.

One of those meaningful experiences took place some years ago when Paul and Karen took her father back to his childhood home. In Paul's words: "Karen thought that it would be a great idea to take her dad and aunt on a road trip to Polo, Illinois to visit their relatives and friends, who were also getting up in age, and to see the changes in their home community. Dad was ninety-two and Karen's aunt was ninety years old and showing early signs of dementia! We thought of many reasons that should have prevented us from making this trip but that 'one last time' seemed to overshadow the doubts. Dad didn't feel he was able to travel anymore. We convinced him that this would work very nicely. He relented and seemed to take a liking to the thought of it.

"But, a week before going—and after all the plans were worked out—Dad again expressed doubts about making the trip! We continued our preparations as though we hadn't heard him. Later, he didn't remember saying that he wasn't going. We made the trip, took our time, all went well, and it turned out to be a very exciting and timely decision to have gone on this adventure. Even though it took a great deal of effort to get this accomplished, the responses from Karen's dad and aunt and the folks in Polo, IL were rich beyond measure! It brought back wonderful memories. We made photo books of their journey which kept the trip alive for them and us." Paul and Karen say that they have "a special peace in their heart and mind" for extending love and care to others and to each other. Their legacy of caregiving will live on.

A slow goodbye

Sanford, Lois, and their children faced a difficult decision. As a result of a severe reaction to chemotherapy for the treatment of his cancer, he spent nearly two months in intensive care at a local hospital and then time in rehab at a nursing care facility. He was offered another form of chemotherapy but was given no guarantee of extending his life or of improving his quality of life. With the support of his family, Sanford decided not to accept the treatment. Instead, he wanted to enjoy whatever remaining time he had, sitting on the deck of his cottage by the river being bathed in nature. He also wanted to be surrounded by his family and friends, not in a sterile medical facility. He would accept the services of a local hospice.

Because his cottage is on a flood plain, the living space and deck are on the second floor. Anticipating the time when he could no longer walk and use the stairs, his son and family friends constructed a ramp to the second floor. When he lost his mobility, his wife Lois was able to take him by wheelchair on various excursions. One trip was to a favorite spot on the Skyline Drive in the Shenandoah National Park in Virginia—a place where they became engaged many years earlier and were now celebrating their fifty-sixth wedding anniversary. This beautiful setting brought back many memories of previous trips there. This is where they loved to hike or just sit on the rocks to watch the sunset.

Another special trip was to a bird sanctuary with longtime friends where he witnessed a flock of seventy thousand snow geese feeding and gathering strength for their journey north. Their steady chant seemed to be a communal blessing as was their occasional flight over him into the afternoon sun. In the midst of the hundreds of other persons at this special gathering, a woman who had attended a retreat facilitated by Sanford stepped forward and took the opportunity to reminisce and to bless him for what he gave to her. She was one of the many persons he nurtured into new levels of spiritual exploration based in part on the work of writer Thomas Merton.

After leaving the gathering of the snow geese, Sanford had enough energy for a stop at an ice cream parlor. Savoring his chocolate ice cream, he turned to his friends and wondered if they needed to leave soon. When they assured him that they were in no hurry he said, "Let's make it a slow goodbye."

As Sanford loses strength and can no longer be on the deck, he now welcomes many friends and family to his river room where, from his bed, he can still see the river and the birds. Some of his conversations are rich in reminiscing about the past. Some are about his approaching death. Sometimes he asks his guests to just sit with him in silence. His example challenges his visitors to reflect on their lives and to pay attention to what is most important.

One daughter who lives about an hour away comes once a week to spend the day together. She is a massage therapist whose touch gives him relief from his suffering. Her husband, a pastor, prays and offers comfort. Their son, who lives close by, provides practical assistance and support regularly. A daughter who lives in California flies across the country often to bring her own special kind of healing. It was a memorable time when all of his children, their spouses, and his five grandchildren gathered around him. He gave each a personal blessing, and they told him the ways he is special to them. There were tears of sadness and joy—but mostly tears of gratitude for these months that they have together as he faces the future. This extended family and community of friends has been enriched by his example and continue to extend his legacy to others.

A closing word

To seniors: As you face your final life stage, do it with courage and with a spirit of expectation. Discover new ideas and purpose. Strengthen your relationships, especially with your spouse and family. Know that some of the best discoveries and the most meaningful ones can happen when you are no longer distracted by careers, attaining, and obtaining. Now is a time to reflect and to genuflect. Humility can be a life-expanding virtue.

Turn to your caregivers with grace and gratitude. Thank them as often as you can. Invite your adult children and other caregivers into your life. You want them to be with you to the end. You need them, and they need you—as partners.

To adult children: Set aside your doubts about whether you are entitled to become a partner with your parents. Just as you needed them when you were young, they need you now, whether they admit that or not. In the midst of your busyness, make time for them. It is an investment in their future—and yours. Most likely, there are some younger eyes and ears that are observing what is happening between you and their grandparents. Just as our values are carried from generation to generation, so is our legacy. Choose your legacy thoughtfully.

Thinking and Planning Ahead

1. How would you describe the common theses from these stories?

2. What part of your legacy do you want to change or expand?

3. What keeps you from sharing personal feelings with those closest to you?

4. How do you think others will experience your legacy?

Endnotes

Chapter 1

1. *Boomers Resource Guide*, "Communicating about Sensitive Subjects."

2. Emily Brandon, "How to Estimate Your Life Expectancy," *U.S. News* (March 21, 2016).

3. Pew Research Center, "Family Support in Graying Societies."

Chapter 3

1. "Social Security," wikipedia.org

2. Merret Mann, "Being a Caregiver to Your Spouse," *Caregivers* (July 17, 2012).

3. Gail Sheehy, *Passages in Caregiving* (New York: HarperCollins, 2011), 51.

Chapter 4

1. Sheehy, *Passages in Caregiving*, 12, 37.

Chapter 5

1. Joe Mont, "Retiring in the Red," *Newsweek* (January 10, 2011), 10.

2. Retirement Industry Trust Association, "Senior Fraud Initiative."

3. Home Instead Senior Care, "The 40-70 Rule" (2010), 13.

4. Christine Benz, "40 Must-Know Statistics About Long Term Care, *Morningstar* (August 9, 2012).

5. Lani Luciano, "The Right Price for Care," *AARP Magazine* (November 16, 2010), 12.

6. Ibid.

7. Karen Jones, *Death for Beginners* (Fresno, CA: Quill Driver Books, 2010), 93.

Chapter 6

1. Walter Brueggemann, *The Land: Place as Gift, Promise, and Challenge in Biblical Faith* (Minneapolis: Fortress Press, 2002), 4.

2. Kimberly J. Stoeckel. "The Role of Home Environments in Residential Adjustment Decision Making in Later Life." Doctor of Philosophy Dissertation, University of Massachusetts, Boston (December 2011), 6–7.

3. Eric Tyson, "Frequently Made Retirement & Estate Planning Mistakes," *EricTyson.com* (May 31, 2010).

4. JanetB (eHow contributor), "The Average Length of Stay in a Skilled Nursing Facility," *eHow*.

Chapter 7

1. Jane E. Brody, "Tackling Care as Chronic Ailments Pile Up," *New York Times* (Feb 21, 2011).

2. Tricia Neuman, Juliette Cubanski, Jennifer Huang, and Anthony Damico. "Rising Costs of Living Longer," *Kaiser Family Foundation* (January 14, 2015).

3. Medco Health Solutions, Inc., "New Survey Shows Seniors Struggle Under Weight of Multiple Medication Use," *PR Newswire* (December 29, 2009).

4. Diana Yates, "The Research Is In: Physical Activity Enhances Cognition, *Illinois News Bureau* (February 18, 2013).

5. Sarah Boseley, "Obesity Causes Premature Death, Concludes Study of Studies," *The Guardian* (July 13, 2016).

6. NIH, "Hearing Loss and Older Adults," *National Institute on Deafness and Other Communication Disorders (NIDCD).*

7. Centers for Disease Control and Prevention, "Important Facts about Falls."

8. AAA, SeniorDriving.AAA.com

Bibliography

Baines, Barry K. *Ethical Wills: Putting Your Values on Paper.* Cambridge, MA: Da Capo Press, 2006.

Casarett, David J. *Last Acts: Discovering Possibility and Opportunity at the End of Life.* New York: Simon & Schuster, 2010.

Chittister, Joan. *The Gift of Years: Growing Older Gracefully.* Katonah, NY: Bluebridge, 2008.

Connidis, Ingrid. *Family Ties and Aging.* Los Angeles: SAGE Publications, Inc., 2009.

Gawande, Atul. *Being Mortal.* New York: Henry Holt & Co., 2014.

Gibbs, Donna. *When I'm 64: The New Retirement.* Sydney: NewSouth Publishing, 2009.

Jones, Karen. *Death for Beginners: Your No-Nonsense, Money-Saving Guide to Planning for the Inevitable.* Fresno, CA: Quill Driver Books, 2010.

Kalanithi, Paul. *When Breath Becomes Air.* London: The Bodley Head-Penguin Random House, 2016.

Miller, Glen E. *Empowering the Patient: How to Reduce the Cost of Healthcare and Improve Its Quality.* Indianapolis: Dog Ear Publishing, 2009.

Miller, Glen E. *Living Thoughtfully, Dying Well.* Harrisonburg, VA: Herald Press, 2014.

Morris, Virginia. *How to Care for Aging Parents.* New York: Workman Publishing, 2014.

Sheehy, Gail. *Passages in Caregiving: Turning Chaos into Confidence.* New York: HarperCollins Publishers, 2011.

Spense, Linda. *Legacy: A Step-by-Step Guide to Writing Personal History.* Athens, OH: Swallow Press, 1997.

Additional Resources

American Association of Retired Persons: www.aarp.com

Audient Alliance for Accessible Hearing Care:
   www.audientalliance.org

CaregiverStress.com: www.caregiverstress.com

Elder Law Associate of Pennsylvania: www.elderlawpa.com

Green Burial Council: www.greenburialcouncil.org

Home Instead Senior Care: www.homeinstead.com

Legacy Center: www.thelegacycenter.com

National Hospice and Palliative Care Organization:
   www.nhpco.org

National Institutes of Health: www.nih.gov

About the Authors

Gerald W. Kaufman was in private practice as a therapist for thirty-four years. He served as a consultant to nursing homes for fifteen years. His Masters in Social Work is from Indiana University.

L. Marlene Kaufman was a therapist in private practice for twenty-four years. Her Masters in Social Work is from Temple University.

Both Gerald and Marlene have dealt extensively with family issues in their practices, including aging and end of life. They offer seminars and workshops on aging issues throughout the US and Canada.

The Kaufmans have co-authored two previous books, *Monday Marriage: Celebrating the Ordinary* and *Freedom Fences: How to Set Limits That Free You to Enjoy Your Marriage and Family*, written with their two daughters.

The Kaufmans have four children and eleven grand-children.

Exhibits

Make as many copies of these forms as your family needs, or go to GoodBooks.com/NecessaryConversations to download printable versions of the forms.

Needs Assessments for Family Helpers

Finances		
Tasks	**Coordinator**	**Provider**
Monitor bill paying		
Review expenses and income		
Balance checkbook		
Review investments and savings		
Review wills		
Review estate planning		

Housing		
Tasks	**Coordinator**	**Provider**
Yard and house maintenance		
Housecleaning		
Assess safety hazards		
Plan for long-term housing		

Health		
Tasks	**Coordinator**	**Provider**
Monitor health changes, nutrition		
Schedule doctor appointments		
Accompany to doctor visits		

Needs Assessments for Family Helpers

Health		
Tasks	**Coordinator**	**Provider**
Monitor medications		
Maintain medical file		

Daily Activities		
Tasks	**Coordinator**	**Provider**
Encourage appropriate social activities		
Provide for transportation needs		
Assess driving skills		
Arrange for personal care services		
Monitor meals and eating habits		
Monitor shopping needs		
Coordinate visitors		

End-of-Life Planning		
Tasks	**Coordinator**	**Provider**
Review Advance Directive, Living Will, and POLST		
Encourage funeral planning		
Make sure will is up to date		
Determine need for and funding of long-term care		

We suggest that adult children/substitutes be given copies of this information and told where the original official documents are kept.

- Names, addresses, phone numbers of family members, including siblings
- Birth and marriage certificates, passports
- Names and contact information of agents of power of attorney and health care proxy
- List of medications currently being taken; list of any allergies (see Exhibit F)
- Health care providers, including doctors and hospital information
- Copy of Medicare or Medicaid card
- Do not resuscitate (DNR) order (see Exhibit E)
- Advance directives (living will, POLST; see Exhibit E)
- Anatomical gift/organ donation card
- Funeral plans

We suggest that parents inform their power of attorney agent(s) and their executor(s) about the secure locations where the following materials can be found.

- Social security number for each parent
- Insurance policies (see Exhibit C)
- Financial information (see Exhibit C)
- Financial statement (see Exhibit D)
- Official financial papers and documents (CDs, stock and bond certificates, annuities paperwork, loans, titles, deeds)
- Computer passwords for all accounts
- Will and testament for each parent

- List of possessions and distribution of them
- Location of the names and account numbers for each of the following, so each can be notified upon the death of the parent directly involved:
  - checking account(s)
  - saving account(s)
  - retirement account
  - annuity(ies)
  - CD(s)
  - mutual funds
  - stocks and bonds
  - life insurance policy(ies)
  - health insurance policy(ies)
  - subscriptions and memberships
  - extended family and friends

Exhibit C
Financial Information

This list is to help you get started and is not exhaustive. Add any other relevant information you feel might be important.

Date: _____

Name of Parent: _____

Address: _____

Phone #: _____

Social security #: _____

Bank lock box location: _____

Bank lock box #: _____

Bank lock box key location: _____

Contents: _____

Lawyer: _____

    Address: _____

    Phone #: _____

Accountant: _____

    Address: _____

    Phone #: _____

Financial advisor: _____

    Address: _____

    Phone #: _____

Exhibit C
Financial Information

Insurance

Life: _____

    Address: _____

    Phone #: _____

    Acct # and value ($): _____

    Contact info: _____

Home & Fire: _____

    Address: _____

    Phone #: _____

    Acct #: _____

    Contact info: _____

Health: _____

    Address: _____

    Phone #: _____

    Acct #: _____

Auto: _____

    Address: _____

    Phone #: _____

    Acct #: _____

Financial Institutions

Banks/credit unions: _____

    Address: _____

    Phone #: _____

    Checking/savings acct #: _____

Exhibit C
Financial Information

Investments

Stocks and Bonds: _____

    Address: _____

    Phone #: _____

    Acct #: _____

Mutual Funds: _____

    Address: _____

    Phone #: _____

    Acct #: _____

Annuities/CDs: _____

    Address: _____

    Phone #: _____

    Acct #: _____

Properties: _____

    Address: _____

    Contact Information: _____

    Acct #: _____

Partnerships: _____

    Address: _____

    Phone #: _____

    Acct #: _____

Exhibit C
Financial Information

Retirement accounts: _____

    Address: _____

    Phone #: _____

    Acct #: _____

Credit Cards: _____

    Phone #: _____

    Acct #: _____

Loans to

Institution or Person: _____

    Address: _____

    Phone #: _____

    Acct #: _____

Loans from

Institution or Person: _____

    Address: _____

    Phone #: _____

    Acct #: _____

Financial Statement

Date: _____

Names: _____

Birth dates: _____

Social security numbers: _____

Addresses: _____

Phone numbers: _____

Assets

Stocks and Bonds: _____

    $ Value: _____

Mutual funds: _____

    $ Value: _____

Partnerships: _____

    $ Value: _____

CDs: _____

    $ Value: _____

Annuities: _____

    $ Value: _____

Retirement accounts: _____

    $ Value: _____

Financial Statement

Checking accounts: _____

   $ Value: _____

Savings accounts: _____

   $ Value: _____

Non-Cash Assets

Properties: _____

   Addresses: _____

   Appraised $ value: _____

Possessions: _____

Life insurance: _____

   Address: _____

   Phone #: _____

   $ value: _____

Liabilities

Loan Amounts: _____

   From: _____

   Interest charged: _____

   Length of term: _____

Net Worth: _____

Medical File

Name: _____

Address: _____

Phone numbers: _____

Contact Person: _____

    Address: _____

    Phone #: _____

Health proxy: _____

    Address: _____

    Phone #: _____

Date: _____

    Blood pressure: _____

    Cholesterol: _____

    Weight: _____

Dates of past illnesses: _____

_____

Dates of hospitalizations: _____

Dates of surgeries: _____

Date: _____

    Present medical conditions: _____

_____

    Symptoms and diagnosis: _____

Health Care Providers and Hospitals

Fill in names, addresses, and phone numbers for each entry.

_____

_____

_____

_____

_____

Pass codes to electronic medical record file maintained by

primary physician/medical practice: _____

Location of copies of Advanced Directive, POLST, and

other legal health care documents: _____

_____

_____

_____

_____

_____

Pass codes to electronic medical record file maintained by

primary physician/medical practice: _____

Location of copies of Advanced Directive, POLST, and

other legal health care documents: _____

Medications and Supplements List

Prescription Medications

Medication	Dosage	Frequency

Non-Prescription Medications and Supplements

_____

_____

_____

_____

_____

_____

_____

_____

Allergies

_____

_____

_____

_____

_____

_____

_____

Senior

I am entrusting you to periodically review my driving safety with me. I will accept your observations without being defensive or blaming other drivers. I will respect your advice to restrict my driving. When the time comes when I can no longer drive, I will give you my keys and permission to sell my vehicle.

Please be gentle with me if I find it difficult to lose this part of my independence.

This is my wish, and I give you permission to make the necessary decisions. Thank you for protecting me. I love you.

Signature: _____ Date: _____

Adult Child/Substitute

I am humbled that you are entrusting me with this responsibility. I love and respect you for preparing with me for the time when it is no longer safe for you to drive. I pledge to be gentle with you as I alert you about my concerns.

My hope is that when the time comes for you to no longer drive, it will be a mutual decision. If I need to make that decision alone, I will do so only to protect you and others.

Please be assured that I will be available to provide transportation or make other arrangements to enable you to remain independent. I am honored and relieved that you have given me this privilege.

Signature: _____ Date: _____

Indicators of Unsafe Driving

- Easily distracted while driving
- Hitting curbs
- Having trouble merging into traffic
- Poor judgment when making left turns and at intersections
- Failing to follow traffic signs and signals
- Near crashes
- Causing dents and scrapes
- Reduced vision/relies on passenger for help
- Responding more slowly to unexpected situations
- Getting lost frequently
- Having a hard time turning around

Adapted from AARP.com

Funeral-Planning Instructions

Funeral home to be contacted: _____

Cemetery: _____

My wishes for remains:

- ☐ Cremated

- ☐ Organ donor

- ☐ Body to science

- ☐ Traditional burial

I would like services held in:

- ☐ Church: _____

- ☐ Funeral Home: _____

- ☐ Other: _____

I request the following person(s) to participate in the service:

- ☐ Pastor: _____

- ☐ Relatives: _____

- ☐ Friends: _____

Scriptures, hymns, poems that are especially meaningful to me :

- ☐ Scriptures: _____

- ☐ Hymns: _____

- ☐ Special music: _____

- ☐ Poems or readings: _____

Funeral-Planning Instructions

Suggestions for Pallbearers (usually six):

1: _____

2: _____

3: _____

4: _____

5: _____

6: _____

My clothing preference: _____

Memorial contributions: _____

Other special instructions: _____

Signature: _____   Date: _____

Adapted from AMC, Akron, PA

Detailed worksheet available at:
deathforbeginners.com